WHAT OTHERS ARE SAYING
ABOUT *LIVING IN TRIUMPH*

"For any person that has struggled with life, this book will help you find practical steps, with God's help to overcome the difficulties that life can throw your way."

Coach Mark Richt, 2023 College Football Hall of Fame Inductee, Former University of Georgia/ University of Miami Head Coach

"I know that with God's help triumph is possible. I hope this book will be helpful for you to overcome whatever you struggle with in your life."

Darryl Strawberry, 4-Time World Series Champion

"God has a plan for our lives to give us hope and a future. My friend Wendell has experienced God's love firsthand and he genuinely desires to see the goodness of God be victorious in your life."

Sonny Sandoval, Lead Singer P.O.D., Co-founder of the Whosoevers, Founder/President of the Youth of a Nation Foundation

"Wow! The principles and concepts revealed in *Living in Triumph* are very impactful. It helped me process thoughts and feelings from personal childhood trauma. I reread multiple paragraphs because I saw myself in the stories. I pray everyone who reads this book takes to heart the words in each chapter. In one way or another your life will never be the same."

LaMorris Crawford, MOL
NFL Chaplain, Author and Speaker

"*Living in Triumph* will help people discover that no matter what challenges they have faced in life you can overcome. Wendell lays it all out there and helps one see how it is possible. He shows you how the choices we make impact how we persevere and overcome. I could not agree with him more on turning to faith in God. From firsthand experience I know the impact hearing from God can make. God transformed my life from a world of brokenness and darkness to healing and happiness. If you are struggling in any area of your life and looking for direction, hope, or answers I strongly encourage you to read *Living in Triumph*."

Erin Merryn, Author, Activist, Founder of Erin's Law

"I have had the honor of knowing Wendell Brown for several years now and the love he has for others is undeniable. His heart for seeing people triumph over their struggles and adversities has motivated him in his ministry, family life, and now in the writing of this book. As you read through *Living in Triumph*, I am positive you will see his heart and his desire for you to overcome the struggles you are facing in this life and you will be more equipped to face them and live in Triumph!"

Kylie Bisutti, author of
I'm No Angel:
From Victoria's Secret Model to Role Model

"Very informative, an authentic guide to restoration of things lost, and leads the reader into the healing arms of Jesus."

Siran Stacy, Former Philadelphia Eagle and All-American Running Back at the University of Alabama, Evangelist & Motivational Speaker

"Wendell Brown cares about people! He has lived his life doing everything he can to help others find productive, fulfilling, faith-filled lives. That's why he wrote this book. He wrote it for you and your friends. Wendell's book has helped me and I am pleased to recommend it to you."

Dr. Bob Broadbooks, Mentor and Friend

"Wendell Brown's gifts and passion for helping struggling people are on full display in this book. While everyone faces challenges in life, some face extreme challenges. For those seeking to turn tragedy into triumph, this book is for you!"

Craig Brown, President & CEO,
Christian Healthcare Ministries

"Wendell Brown has been a champion for people who are deeply wounded. He offers a framework to understand the pain of the past, namely receptive, responsible, and reactive struggles. From this, the reader can begin to identify choices that he/she has in the present and this leads to a sense of hope. As a faith-based book, it offers food for the journey."

Jim L. Smith, D.Min.
Professor Emeritus, Ohio Christian University

"I always tell my clients....'We all have choices in life'. We can focus on the negative or the positive. We can live as a victim or in victory. We can allow struggles to define us or we can live triumphant. *Living in Triumph* shows us that through our faith in God we will have hope, healing, and restoration. I cannot wait to share this book with my clients."

Jaime Hampton, LPCC, CCTP
Dynami Counseling, LLC

LIVING IN TRIUMPH

WENDELL BROWN

LIVING
IN
TRIUMPH

FINDING FREEDOM
FROM THE STRUGGLES OF LIFE

WENDELL BROWN

Published by HigherLife Publishing & Marketing, Inc.
PO Box 623307
Oviedo, FL 32762
AHigherLife.com

Cover and Interior Design by Faithe Thomas, Master Design Marketing, LLC

ISBN (Paperback): 978-1-958211-38-0
ISBN (Ebook): 978-1-958211-39-7
Library of Congress # 1-12255400901

Printed in the United States of America.

10 9 8 7 6 5 4 3 2 1

DEDICATION

This book would not be possible without the support and encouragement of our Tragedy Into Triumph team (T.D., Daryl, Chuck, Steve, Tim), who were extremely influential and helpful in bringing it to publication. I am so thankful for each of you and the partnership we share together. Your faith in Christ and big-picture thinking are so valuable to me.

Thank you to my great friend, Siran Stacy. You inspire me with every conversation to be a better person. Thank you to Zach for always being in my corner. Thank you to Keith for asking me the tough questions. Thank you to Jerry for speaking wisdom in my life.

Thank you to my mother for modeling what it means to love others.

Thank you to my NCO District family. You each mean so much to me. I count it an honor to serve with you.

Additionally, thank you to everyone who has encouraged me to write this book. There are so many people who have believed in me through the years; however, no one has encouraged me more than my wife, Tammi. Thank you for being my source of strength, and thank you for choosing to journey through life with me; you bring me great joy. It is your belief in me that has brought me where I am today, and without your confidence these words would never have been written.

Thank you also to my wonderful children: Emma, Abigail, Grace, and Christian. I hope that you will always find a way to live in triumph everyday of your life.

CONTENTS

INTRODUCTION

I have always admired overcomers and their stories of triumph. These individuals surmount immense difficulties in spite of statistics, adversity, limitations, or even expert commentary to realize something great in their lives. Amazing! From the "Miracle on Ice" to the successful "Hail Mary" pass, we all love stories of overcoming. From the walk-on player that becomes the star quarterback to the person reading at an eighth-grade level that applies themselves and earns two degrees, I love hearing stories and meeting people who find ways to be victorious in life. I am astounded at how a person can be diagnosed with terminal cancer, yet find a way to be filled with joy. I am inspired by the person who grew up with nothing yet finds a way to build a corporation. The drive, the commitment, and the work ethic displayed in every example amazes me. It's partly because I have overcome a few obstacles in my own life that these stories resonate within me. Some of my obstacles were the result of my own poor choices, but others existed through no fault of my own. Nevertheless, they were obstacles. And they were real. If anyone knows that, I do.

How's this for a list of qualifications for overcoming hardship? In my life, I have done all of the following: I have struggled with addiction. I have completed U.S. Army paratrooper school while sick. I have been ambushed at gunpoint with a 9mm placed against my temple. We were told our daughter was not supposed to live. A horrific car accident left me permanently scarred. Those are just a few examples.

I authored this book because I want you to succeed. If you picked up this book on a whim, or just liked the title, or it was a gift, I want you to know that I am in your corner. You should know though, that this book is not about my obstacles, nor is it about the obstacles of others. To focus our attention on the obstacles leaves us wondering if there is any hope for our own lives. No, this book is about how we triumph, and how to live "in triumph." What do we need to believe about ourselves? What do we need to believe about others? How do we make decisions? How do we have hope? How do we *sustain* that hope?

> **I AUTHORED THIS BOOK BECAUSE I WANT YOU TO SUCCEED.**

This book is meant to provide the tools we need to get through life's struggles when they come—because they will come. When they do, we must have strong core beliefs and a plan of action to successfully get us through. There is a real possibility that a good portion of you reading this book will encounter obstacles before you even finish it! How will you respond?

Introduction

What will determine your success? What must you do to become a victor instead of a victim?

Will you find real hope and help so you can rise above? That is completely dependent on you. It is my goal that somehow after reading this book, you will be inspired to live life to its fullest. You are going to make mistakes, and it won't be easy, but you can do it! I want you to discover that your life need not be dictated to you by other people or by circumstances, but instead can be *directed* by—YOU! Triumph is possible, and available for every person on the face of the earth.

I promise to be with you every step of the way and have written this as though I am right there with you as you read and process it. It will take some time as we work together. Some concepts may seem simple, others practical, and others may challenge your present thinking about yourself or your life.

So, let's commit to some real work and take a journey together! Are you ready? I am. I have been waiting a long time for you to read this.

CHAPTER 1

THE STRUGGLE IS REAL

AL grew up in a home that was anything but functional. His father drank and was abusive, both mentally and physically. Imagine seeing your father pointing a gun at your mother, and proclaiming that he was going to kill her. That was the world this little boy found himself in when he was just nine years old. He did the only thing a little boy his age knew to do. He ran three blocks over to get his grandmother and frantically told her what was happening. The two of them rushed back only to hear the pop of the gun as they entered the house to discover that his father had shot and killed his mother.

Al was placed in the care of his uncle, but that was not a stable environment either. His uncle possessed the same abusive nature as his father. When Al was twelve, the uncle told him to get out of his house and that is exactly what Al did. He packed his clothes in two paper bags and set out on his own thinking that anywhere was better than where he was. At a young age, he learned what it was like to bounce from place to place, and he never knew the love, support, and nurturing that should have been given to a young child who had endured so much trauma.

He spent many nights alone and afraid. There were nights he would sleep in a junkyard. Other nights he would stay with friends. He turned himself in to Child Protective Services only to run away three weeks later. Finally, he was put in a boys' home, only to have his aunt and uncle take him into their care again, and once again be physically abused by his uncle. In Al's own words, "I wish they would have left me in the boys' home!"

By the age of eighteen, Al had experienced more heartbreak, loss, and difficulty than most people do in a lifetime, yet if you met Al today, you would never know it.

Today, he has a successful business, a beautiful family, and is the proudest granddad you could ever meet. What brought about this transformation? How was he able to *not* repeat the cycle of abuse and alcoholism that he knew? What internal change prevented him from ending up like his uncle, and instead, being one of the kindest men you could ever meet? Those are all great questions. I hope as you read this book you will discover the answer.

It is remarkable to consider how one individual could overcome such incomprehensible odds. Many people struggle with circumstances that may not seem as large to the casual observer, but for that person are insurmountable. The struggle is literally real for everyone. Perhaps you have a story like Al's or maybe your story is entirely different. Every person on earth faces adversity at some point. Some may face more than others. Everyone will struggle with something. Adversity is different for each of us, but its severity, its exact effect, is dependent on how each person processes the experience.

It is at this point in the beginning of the book that I want to remind you that this book is not necessarily about the various kinds of struggles. This book is more about *overcoming* struggle. However, for us to ensure we move forward correctly, we do need to define the different types of struggles that we face in our lives. This may be the most tedious work we will do in this book, but we need to do it to en-

> IDENTIFYING THE STRUGGLE CAN HELP US DETERMINE A RESPONSE

sure that we understand ourselves in the midst of a struggle. Identifying the struggle can help us determine a response, so this step is necessary. Don't go to sleep on me yet! I promise we will work though this in due time. And best of all, the journey will be worth it.

What is your struggle? People often respond with something like: *I struggle with anxiety or depression.* Or *I struggle with addiction.* Or *I struggle with my marriage.* Each of these is certainly a struggle, but let's simplify our thinking a bit by placing them into different categories. There are actually three types of adversity that need to be identified in our lives. The first type comes from circumstances, places, and actions against us that are out of our control. We will call this *receptive struggle.*

Receptive Struggle

The situation Al experienced was a receptive struggle. He didn't ask to be born into that family. He had no control over his violent and alcoholic father. He couldn't change where he grew up or what happened to him as a child. He couldn't protect his mother. The trouble in his life was thrust upon him by the decisions and the struggles of others. Receptive struggle is difficult to overcome because of one simple, but extremely challenging, question: *Why?* The question hangs in the air like an indictment. And like a legal charge, how you answer affects your life forever. Why did this happen to me? Why would someone do this to me? Why didn't they stop this? Why didn't they see what it was doing? You didn't cause it, you couldn't change it, yet here you are receiving the brunt of someone else's struggle. Receptive struggle can be so damaging to our own sense of value and worth because most of the time (but not always), it is those closest to us that hurt us. It is not fair to you, but it is yours nonetheless. Their decisions have become such a barrier in your life that you wonder how you are going to manage.

There are all kinds of receptive struggles that people experience. Many reading this book have been abused, or lost family member(s) to a drunk driver. Some have had a spouse that cheated on them or have trusted someone with an investment, only to have that person defraud them. It's feasible that life was good for you until that person stabbed you in the back at work and took credit for your idea and stole the promotion that was rightfully yours. You were doing just fine until that person hurt you deeply. There are countless examples, but they all have one thing in common.

Receptive struggle forces us into a defensive position as others hurt us, and in the process, it chips away at our confidence, challenging the core of our being. It has a taxing effect on what we believe about ourselves and others. Along with the *why* questions come the *what ifs*. It's at this point where we can start to believe that *we* are responsible for whatever happened to us. *What if I had responded differently? What if I had avoided that conversation?*

> **MAKE NO MISTAKE THOUGH, YOU ARE NOT RESPONSIBLE.**

What if I were not in their life—maybe they would be happier if I were not? Make no mistake though, you are not responsible. This happened to you. You didn't create it. Receptive struggle is like the gift you didn't want that keeps on giving. It can be overcome, but that requires retraining our heart and mind in what we believe and how we process all of it.

I wish it were the only struggle you will ever face, but it's not. The next one is *responsible struggle*.

Responsible Struggle

In this one, there is no one to blame but yourself. You are the one responsible for these circumstances in your life. You took the first drag of a cigarette and now you are addicted to nicotine. You gave into pressure and snorted that first line, and now you can't seem to get through the day without it. You compromised, decided it was worth the risk, and now you are unhappy and have been divorced three times. You decided that your car didn't need an oil change for 100,000 miles and now you need a new engine. You committed the crime and now it is your responsibility to do the time.

Responsible struggle usually begins with *one small compromise*, which leads to increasingly larger ones over time. Each compromise gets easier and easier the more we settle. One day we wake up and look at our situation, and wonder how we got there. Our compromises become easier over time because responsible struggle leads to low self-esteem. We start to believe a narrative that goes something like this: *Because I have done x, no one will respect me. I have made so many awful decisions and I know I am a horrible person, so it doesn't matter if I do this too. I have already failed so miserably. Who cares at this point?*

Responsible struggle can be overcome. However, our toughest critic is our own voice that lives rent free in our head. The greatest barrier to overcoming responsible struggle is our own guilt. Additionally, the wreckage it leaves behind is a constant reminder of our failure, which speaks repeatedly: *You did this; no one will trust you again. You really messed up this time; they will never believe you again. Wait until everyone finds out about this; they will never ask you to participate again.* These statements become oft-repeated phrases in our head like the tune of a song that never leaves our minds. Responsible struggle places us in a position of doubt as the value we had is eroded by the decisions we have made.

Again, I wish this was the last struggle, but there is still one more. The final struggle is *reactive struggle*.

Reactive Struggle

These are the ones in which you are forced to react. They seem to have no reason, but catch you off guard, perhaps because they feel random or a part of the cycle of life that affects us all. What is so unique about them is that they just happen. There's no one to blame; they are simply the result of living on planet Earth. The deer that runs out in front of us from nowhere on the interstate. The tree that falls and hits the corner of our house in a storm. The traffic jam on the way to work when we are already running behind. The phone call that a close friend has passed away unexpectedly. The news in the doctor's office at your yearly checkup that brings you to your knees. In all these cases, you are the recipient of a struggle that you did not produce. This was not a trial brought about by someone else either. You are forced to react to an external event or circumstance that just happened to you, and you cannot pinpoint a reason for it. When reactive struggle finds us, it is important to remember that every person on the face of the earth must endure reactive struggles. They are a part of normal life.

The danger though with reactive struggle is the damage it can inflict on our attitude or the other people in our lives. The stress it causes can transform your life in a negative way. Suddenly you are interacting with those closest to you in frustration because of the circumstances you are in. Often these struggles are a hindrance to joy in our lives. These troubles are one more item that must be dealt with, one more obstacle that must be overcome. In dealing with reactive struggle, we can find ourselves withdrawing and stopping all other interactions. We put our interests on hold to deal with the moment, not realizing that life is so much more than our immediate struggles.

So, there you have it: receptive struggle, responsible struggle, and reactive struggle. Consider the struggles you have/had in your life. Which kind are they? Process how each one originated in your life. List them below.

Receptive Struggle

_____

_____

_____

_____

_____

Responsible Struggle

_____

_____

_____

_____

_____

Reactive Struggle

_____

_____

_____

_____

_____

Identifying the struggle is hugely important, as it can change how we react in the moment. Recognizing the type of struggle also can provide the pathway for us to find our way through it successfully. The first step in conquering any problem in our lives is to determine its cause. Determining the cause positions us for success as we establish a starting point to begin the work. Let me provide an illustration for each one.

The Receptive Struggle: Repeating the Cycle

What is the cause? Is it trauma in someone else's life? Is it their situation, their background, or history? Did they have a bad day and are taking it out on you? Are you the recipient of their ongoing fight with addiction? It's natural and normal that we receive from others because we were created for connection. We're supposed to interact with others. The problem comes when we repeat the cycle because we did not take the time to process the effects of our past hurts. What do I mean? Living with the effects of another's struggle can teach us to follow the same pattern in our own lives. That's how dysfunctional patterns get passed along to the next generation. If left unresolved, it will be far too easy to default to the behaviors that have been modeled for us. It is vitally important for us to recognize the cause of the struggle we were in, so that we do not make that problem our own. If we do not recognize the source, we will be quick to repeat it. Understanding that a problem originates in someone else provides a way for us to stop a behavior before we repeat it.

Here's a quick example from my own life: I was having a terrible week. Life at this point was difficult for me and I was working quite a bit. There had been one fire after another to put out as I worked with the individuals of the organization I was leading at the time. I came home for supper one night to find that my young children were fighting, and needed me to moderate. (This was one of the worst moments I had as a parent.) I slammed my hand on the table and with a raised voice said, "I listen to everyone's problems all day long! The last thing I want to do is listen to yours when I get home." Silence reigned for a split second. No sooner did I get those words out of my mouth when I realized what I had done and asked my family to forgive me.

What happened? My problems at work were so great that they immediately caused a receptive struggle for my family. The difficulty I was dealing with during the day had nothing to do with what was happening in the five minutes I had been home. It would have been easy for my wife to respond in anger at my outburst. It would have been easy to punish my children for doing nothing more than being children, and cause greater issues for them later in their lives as their father took out his frustrations on them. That situation could have been much worse than it was, and believe me, it was not great. Recognizing what I was doing caused me to ask my family for forgiveness. I have spent so much of my life processing struggles; even so, I was not immune to them. We never are. My wife, Tammi, realizing the source of my stress did not repeat the cycle and raise her voice. I am so thankful that the situation did not escalate.

The Responsible Struggle: Choices Have Consequences

We are all free moral agents. It's important to remember that. We have choices. In this case, you ask yourself who is to blame for a continual problem in your life, and the finger on your hand points back at you. You caused it and you have no one else to blame. You have been given the gift of free will. Even though circumstances and events shape our lives and make us prone toward certain behaviors, *we still make the choice*. We must recognize this and take responsibility for our actions because these negative cycles can be changed through our own grit and determination. We do literally have the power to say no. We do have the ability to learn and change our behavior. We can best work through responsible struggle by making a different choice. For example, if you struggle with gambling, and you are tempted every day when you pass a casino on your way home from work, make a different choice. Find another route home that avoids the casino. Your choice has power in helping you overcome obstacles. Once we admit we are to blame, and make a firm commitment to change, we begin to prevail over responsible struggle immediately. This can be extremely difficult to do, but when it is hard to choose differently, those closest to us can help and hold us accountable. More importantly, when we are weak, there is strength available from God if we ask Him. I cannot wait to talk to you more about that later in the book.

The Reactive Struggle: Out of the Blue

How did this happen? If you don't know, then you are experiencing reactive struggle. When there is seemingly no cause, you must recognize that so you can maintain control of your emotions. The surest way to overcome reactive struggle is to accept that *bad things happen to good people all the time.* If there is no one to blame, then our response must be to adapt and march on. Things happen as a result of living on planet Earth. Accept it! You may think that you've had your fair share of problems already. Everyone has! You can let reactive struggle defeat you, or you can defeat it. It is that simple. I know that everyone is looking for reassurance, and I understand that everyone is trying to find the easiest and best way to maintain their comfort level, but a different approach is necessary if we are truly going to rise above this struggle. *Consider this: Either we become comfortable with change or we remain uncomfortable.* Not one thing in your life is going to stay the same—ever. Time,

> CONSIDER THIS: EITHER WE BECOME COMFORTABLE WITH CHANGE OR WE REMAIN UNCOMFORTABLE.

circumstances, and people are constantly changing. The moment we accept that life doesn't stay the same is the moment we start appreciating the present. When we appreciate the present, we become expectant and grateful for the way things are, instead of trying to make every moment the same. When we accept change as a constant, we can begin to find comfort, even in the midst of turmoil. Accept that things are going to change, and you just might find the comfort and peace needed to overcome reactive struggle.

The best way to illustrate this point is to experience it. Try this. At your next gathering with family or friends, make the conscious decision to *be in the moment*. Put down your phone and other distractions and focus on your company. Live in the moment. Recognize that this moment will never be repeated. It's fleeting, so savor it. Enjoy it, and you will find that you begin to appreciate all of your moments far more than you ever did before. This will actually increase your joy overall. A similar course helps when times are difficult. Recognize that this moment will also never be repeated. Be intentionally thankful that tomorrow is a different day. It will not last forever. When we become comfortable with change it actually allows us to find contentment in the moment.

Overcoming any type of struggle starts with identifying which it is. This allows us to process how we need to respond, but that's just the beginning. There is much more we need to understand about ourselves if we are going to live above struggles. We also need to understand what we believe. Before we move on, I should warn you that the next chapter might meddle in your life a bit. Its purpose is to cause you to reflect on your core beliefs and why they are there. If you are okay with that, then turn the page; if you're not, turn the page anyway out of curiosity. Seriously, aren't you a little curious?

CHAPTER 2

WHAT DO YOU BELIEVE?

My wife, Tammi, and I first met Amanda in connection with a community kids' choir that we were putting together. If ever there was a talented young lady, it was Amanda. She was smart, and oh, could she sing. She was a natural leader, and the other children loved being around her. Her only problem was that she came from a troubled home. She was an only child, but her mother had her when she was fourteen. Amanda was thirteen when my wife and I came into her life, which meant her mother was still only twenty-seven and unmarried. Men came and went in Amanda's home life. None of them were there for very long because their relationships with her mother never seemed to last. Amanda watched as her mother struggled with men and addiction. We didn't know what words were spoken to Amanda at home, but once when we picked her up, we stood in the door waiting for her and we were amazed at what we saw inside. The floor of the apartment was covered in trash: fast food wrappers, beer bottles, cigarette butts, and other garbage littered the floor and appeared to have been there for days. We waited at the door and noticed that Amanda looked fearful that we were there. Her mother was on one couch, her boyfriend on the other. They were watching two TVs—one stacked on top of the other and both were on different channels with the volume up. Amanda greeted us with a quick, "Just a minute, I will be right out." As soon as she uttered those words, her mother turned slowly to look at me, eyes glazed over and red, a beer in her hands, and said, "She is not going to be able to come today. She has to clean her room." Amanda begged and pleaded with her mother that the whole house was a mess and that she would help clean not just her room but all of it if she could go, but her mother was adamant. I tried to voice support, but it was to no avail. We remember leaving her home and feeling sad for her, wondering what was going to happen to her. What was really happening in her home life? What words were being spoken into her life? *She had to clean her room tonight for some reason, yet trash covered the entire living room and her mother was too high to care,* I thought angrily as we walked away.

Amanda lived in a part of town that was .5 percent away from being the worst crime neighborhood in a large community. We received that statistic from the police department just days before our visit. To say this was a rough area was an understatement. Drugs, prostitution, alcoholism, and theft were everywhere. If people moved to this area, they didn't stay if they could get out, yet here was talented Amanda.

After that encounter with her mother, we showed extra love to Amanda. I remember my wife, Tammi, telling her what an amazing young lady she was. She shared with Amanda that she thought she was quite gifted. Tammi told her that she could do anything she wanted. All she had to do was believe. Tammi suggested she go to college and encouraged her to work hard toward that goal, sharing that scholarships could pay for it. We will never forget Amanda's response: "Tammi, don't you know that girls like me don't get to go to college? When I get older, I will be doing the same thing everyone else does around here."

Stop and think about that for a minute. At thirteen years of age, this young girl had a firm belief about her life. It was already decided. She believed there was no changing what was already set in motion for her. We tried repeatedly to speak against that mentality in her life, but we did not break through. I wish I had a different ending to this story, but I don't. She ended up letting all her talent and intelligence and her vigor in life fade as she settled for the lie that girls like her don't get to have the great things in life. When I reflect upon her story and how a good life was taken from her based on a false premise, my heart breaks. The struggle for Tammi and me was that we set the table for her. Yet, somewhere along the way, she believed something that wasn't true.

What about you, what do you believe? You see, what we believe shapes our behavior. What we believe determines our outcome. What we believe gives us confidence or fear. Seriously, what do you believe?

What determines your success or failure in this life is not centered on each day's circumstances. Instead, it is absolutely centered on the things you believe. In fact, there are three areas of belief that we must come to grips with in relation to our lives. These areas are so vital that without a clear understanding in each of them, there is no opportunity to flourish. We will never find freedom from struggle in our lives until we settle our belief system. If you are not sure what you believe, I am here to help. If you know what you believe, we will ensure that you have a proper understanding in three foundational areas. We will focus on each of them with a question.

> **WE WILL NEVER FIND FREEDOM FROM STRUGGLE IN OUR LIVES UNTIL WE SETTLE OUR BELIEF SYSTEM.**

1. What do you believe about purpose?

2. What do you believe about yourself?

3. What do you believe about others?

Purpose

Is there a purpose for your life? Take that a step further: Is there a purpose for every person on earth? Your answer to this question is fundamental in establishing your belief system. Do you believe there is meaning and purpose for human existence? How you answer that question will determine the way you live your life. How you answer that question will determine the decisions you make in this life. If purpose is absent from life, it doesn't matter what we do. If there is purpose, then decisions are important. If there is purpose, then your life has significance.

What Do You Believe?

We'll define *purpose* as the reason for which something exists. Let's ask the same question a different way. Is there a reason for your existence? Ponder this question. Take a moment and reflect on your life. This might be a good moment to pull out a pen and write down what you think. I asked the publisher to insert space here, so you can write in the book if you like. Who are you as a person? This is an important question in your life. It is something you have to settle deep within your spirit.

_____

_____

_____

_____

_____

This chapter is so important to overcoming struggle that you need to take your time. So, please do not rush through it. If you are in a hurry right now, or are mentally preoccupied about something else, put this aside and wait until you can give it your full attention. Is there a reason for your existence? Let's pause for just a moment so you can reflect. Think about your life. What do you truly believe in your heart? Consider the good and the bad. Encapsulate your interactions with others. Do you believe you add value to life? Close your eyes if necessary. Take your time. Go get another cup of coffee, and take as much time as you need. I'll be right here waiting for you when you return.

You made it back. Great! Trust me about this. Your answer to this question determines so much in your life. Get ready to write the answer: Yes or No. You can only choose one; there is no middle ground. Here comes the large font!

Is there a reason for your existence?

According to the Cato 2019 Welfare, Work, and Wealth National Survey, 83% of Americans would say yes to that question and 16% would answer no.[1]

For those that answered no, it is okay. Truly, it is. I want to help you! I need to confess that there are limitations in a book. There is only so much we can accomplish with words on a page, but work through this exercise with me anyway. I want you to think about the people that matter to you. Who are they? I don't know your home life or how you were raised. I don't know the circumstances surrounding your life. I would not pretend for one second that I have walked in your shoes. However, I would venture a guess that there is someone you know on a personal level that means something to you. Perhaps they are a parent, a friend, a teacher, a relative, a neighbor, a coach, or someone else that is important in your life. Why they are important, only you know.

Please write their name here: _____

---

1 Emily Ekins, "What Americans Think About Poverty, Wealth, and Work," What Americans Think About Poverty, Wealth, and Work (Cato. org, 2019), https://www.cato.org/sites/cato.org/files/2019-09/Cato2019WelfareWorkWealthSurveyReport%20%281%29.pdf.

Bigger question. Why do they matter to you? They matter to me because:

_____

_____

Now let's reverse it. Who do you matter to?

Many people feel as if no one would miss them. Many people believe that they have nothing relevant to offer others, and because of this, there is no meaning to their existence. However, that is *never* the case. I know this because you listed someone that matters to you. For them to be special to you means you have had some type of interaction with them. There was a conversation, there was an act of kindness, or they showed up when you needed them the most. They impacted your life. Your life is part of their life's story. If that is the case, then your life has impacted them. Whether you feel it or not. The sheer fact that they matter to you means that your life has had an impact on their life too. You may feel like your life hasn't had a positive impact on the person you mentioned above. You may feel like the reciprocation of kindness from you fell short, but whether that interaction was positive or negative isn't relevant. This is relevant: You impacted someone else's life. If you have the power to impact another human being, there must be a purpose for you. You can argue that you are not living up to your purpose.

IF YOU HAVE THE POWER TO IMPACT ANOTHER HUMAN BEING, THERE MUST BE A PURPOSE FOR YOU.

I will grant you that discovering purpose can seem daunting at times. However, difficulty in discovering purpose does not mean it is nonexistent.

Consider this: If we can impact someone else's life, how can there not be purpose behind that impact? What good does it do to have an effect on someone without considering the purpose behind the effect?

Okay, that was deep stuff. Are you ready? All you have to do is acknowledge that there is purpose. So now, let me ask that question again and this time I will let you circle the answer.

Is there a reason for your existence? Yes! <— Circle this!

Now that we have established that you have a purpose for your life, there is a follow-up question. If there is purpose, where did it come from? I know what you are thinking: *Enough with the questions already!* Sorry, but we must answer this question too. Where did your purpose come from? Did the cosmic universe accidently cause purpose to happen, or is there a greater meaning? Were you were created *on purpose?*

Look, there is a lot of confusion in our world today. There is much debate about life and its origin. There are conversations surrounding religion, and its positive or negative impact on the world. I am certainly not speaking of religion here. We don't need to look at religion to find this answer. Religions throughout history are going to answer the purpose question in many different ways, and at times, religion can lead us astray instead of home. Depending on what religion you follow you can answer this question in many ways. However, only one of them is true. The interesting point to consider is that each of us must answer this question *on our own*. Every person reading this book will have to answer this question for themselves. It is your life. So, where did your purpose come from?

If there is purpose in your life now, that means there was purpose in your beginning. When you first entered the world, and took your first breath, you began to pursue your purpose and you didn't even know it. If there was purpose in your beginning, then someone or something placed that purpose into your life, and it was not an accident. There is no such thing as accidentally on purpose. Now, if there was purpose in your beginning, can we not also conclude that there is purpose in your end?

The ancients referred to God as the Alpha and Omega. That means the beginning and the end. Alpha is the first Greek letter and Omega is the last. If we take that literally, it means that God was at your beginning and God will be at your end, and yet it is so much more than that. The ancients believed that God was not merely at the beginning of everything, but that God exists through all of time and that He will be at the end as well. They were literally declaring that God has always been and always will be. I know that it is not fashionable today to talk this way, but I think we should. What good does it do us to claim there is purpose, and not understand the One who gave that purpose to us in the first place?

If God has always been, if God always will be, then that must mean that He is here now. He is present. Stop and ponder that, as you read this book. God is existing in time right now with you. If He is here now, and if He has always existed, then He must know some things about the universe. He must know some things about what is happening in our world. *He must know some things about you.* If He is going to be in your end, then there must be some concepts He wants to teach you, some lessons He wants you to learn, some actions He wants you to take.

This would be a great place to put the book down, and just say a prayer. Understanding purpose is so important that it will overshadow everything else in this book. Put the book down, and just exist in the presence of God. Ask Him to show Himself to you. Ask Him to allow you to sense His presence. Ask Him to be real in your life. Whether you feel it or not, tell Him you would like to know Him deeply. Tell Him you would like to see evidence of Him. Ask Him to help you discover your purpose. Tell Him you don't have all the answers. Tell Him how you feel. Ask Him questions. Say whatever comes to your mind and heart, and then wait on Him. You may need to take some time, *some real time*, to speak to Him and allow Him to speak to you. I don't know how long it will take in your life, but this is the moment that I am trusting God will come through for you.

Here is my promise to you: He will speak to you, but you need to pay attention. There will be a tug at your heart. There will be a feeling. Something will come to mind. There *will be* a moment! Rest in that moment. Enjoy His presence with you. Take as long as you need. I will be here when you get back. I can't wait for you to hear from Him! If you need help getting started with this, here is a sample prayer, and some room to write your thoughts:

God, would You come into my life and help me discover purpose? I ask forgiveness for anything I have done and want to have a relationship with You. Would You come into my heart and walk the journey of life with me? I would love to have Your Spirit speak to me. Thank You! In Jesus' name, Amen!

How did you feel? What do you think He said to you? Take a moment and write down any thoughts you had or anything you sensed God saying to you.

_____

_____

_____

_____

_____

_____

_____

_____

Wasn't that great? There is nothing better than asking for help from the One who was at the beginning and will be at the end. There can be no true positive momentum in your life until you ask God for help.

The next question we need to answer is:

What do you believe about yourself?

When you think about your positive or negative impact on the world and others, what do you think? What voices have you heard in your life? If you truly know me, you will discover that I love to have fun and joke around. I learned one day at an early age that I could make people laugh in class, and on that fateful day, I quit going to school for an education and started going to have fun! In eighth grade, I was acting like my normal self and made a joke in class. My teacher replied with: "Wendell, you have diarrhea of the mouth." The entire class erupted in laughter at her words about me. In the moment I acted as if I didn't care, but I did care. It impacted me. I thought about it when I got home. I pondered those words. It hurt! I got over it, but that one phrase was monumental enough in my life that I still think about it at times. Those words took maybe two to three seconds to utter, but I still think about them thirty plus years later!

Obviously, I do not believe I have diarrhea of the mouth or you wouldn't be reading this book, but I must admit that the impact of that moment has been a hurdle for me at various times. Do you know why that is? Because words spoken to us and about us shape the perceptions we have about ourselves.

What has been spoken to you? What words have shaped your thinking? How have those words affected your life? Did you accept them as truth? My father was haunted for much of his life by words that his mother said to him. She said, "I wish you had never been born." He ran to his room, expecting his mother to apologize but she never did. I saw firsthand how that statement impacted my father. Perhaps some of you have heard those exact words in your life. Or, phrases like these play back in your head: *I have never loved you. You ruined my day. I wish we would have never met. You are not smart enough. You will never change. You can't do it. You will always be a drunk. You will always be worthless. You will never amount to anything. Once a liar, always a liar. No one likes you. You will always be a cheat. I hate you. I don't even know why you exist. You always do it wrong. You never help me. You will never help anyone.*

> **A FEW WORDS SPOKEN IN JUST SECONDS CAN HAVE A LASTING EFFECT ON YOUR BELIEF SYSTEM.**

There's no denying that words spoken to us can have a lasting effect. They hurt. They cut us deeply. A few words spoken in just seconds can have a lasting effect on your belief system. It's bad enough when the words are spoken once, but those spoken repeatedly can set a course for self-destruction as they can morph our perception about ourselves into a new reality. If we hear something long enough we will begin to accept it as truth! However, it's important for us to understand that *words are NOT always true.* People use words to manipulate, lie, or make themselves appear better than they are. Words spoken in anger and thoughtlessness may have no merit whatsoever. Some words reflect someone else's position and are only spoken into your life because that other person refuses to change. *Words can speak truth, but they are not always true.* As you consider the words that have been spoken over your life, remember that. Some of the words spoken to you were the result of receptive struggle and were inflicted on you because of someone else's issue or pain. Recognize that.

Perhaps as you reflect on the words spoken over your life, you discover that a portion of them were true. I have good news for you! Every person has made their fair share of mistakes. Every person has had moments we wish we could get back. Wishing for a "redo" is the pinnacle reminder in your life that you are not what people have said about you. Wishing to change something about your life is the surest proof that you are different than what someone else said or believes.

Perhaps you have lived out some of the statements about you. Perhaps for a time you were a liar. Perhaps you were a cheat. Perhaps you were a drunk. That was then, this is now. Those moments do not define purpose because that moment is now in your past. To fulfill our purpose, we step into the reason we were created, and choose to make better decisions the next time. Remember, purpose is the reason for which something exists. God created you, so He is the reason you exist, and all His purposes are good. He didn't create you to be a liar or a drunk or a thief. He gave you His purpose. The only way the past is repeated is if you let it. The only way to ensure history doesn't repeat itself is to make a change.

Since there is meaning and purpose to your life, that means there is something to learn from every mistake. Because you have purpose, you *can* learn; and if you can learn, you are "smart enough." If you don't repeat a mistake, then I guess you "*can change*." Many of you have believed things about your life that aren't true. Some of you have allowed your past mistakes to shape your life for a long time now. Don't let your past define your future anymore. Let them go and make a change. Others have allowed words to shape their belief system. It is time to let those words go too. It is time to make a change. You were created on purpose, with purpose, and for purpose. I think you need to hear that again. You were created on

> **YOU WERE CREATED ON PURPOSE, WITH PURPOSE, AND FOR PURPOSE.**

purpose, with purpose, and for purpose! If you have struggled in this area of life, please understand this fundamental truth: The only course of action that validates the words spoken over you is to do nothing about them. You decide what you listen to and believe.

One more thought about words. If you have said negative words like those above to someone else in anger, you need to seek their forgiveness. If you have belittled someone to make yourself feel better (or look better), you need to change that behavior and seek forgiveness. Too often, we want to point fingers at what others are guilty of doing to us and forget what we are guilty of doing to others. If you have spoken words in haste and have not sought forgiveness, this is the time! Make a list below. Please do not let words spoken in haste shape someone else's belief system. Don't wait! If something came to mind, if a person or circumstance entered your thoughts, take care of it. Set up an appointment with them. Text them, call them, email them. Just reach out to seek their forgiveness. (List as many or as few names as you need to.)

I need to ask _____

to forgive me for _____ .

I need to ask _____

to forgive me for _____ .

I need to ask _____

to forgive me for _____ .

This leads us to our last belief question that needs answered.

What do you believe about others?

We have established that there is purpose in your life. That means there is purpose in every human life. Every person. Every life. Period. There are no exceptions. Whether they live up to their purpose is their decision, but central to our belief about ourselves is the belief that every life can have purpose. There are some vile people on earth, who have done terrible things. Even so, fundamental to our own ability to overcome our struggles is the understanding that it is possible for anyone to change. We also understand that the individual is the only one who can choose to change. Only we can decide to step into the purpose God would realize in us. Since there is purpose in every life, then there is undiscovered significance in every interaction we have with others. It would be incredibly selfish for us to believe that we can have a future despite our past, but others cannot. It's only fair to pass the same courtesy we apply to ourselves on to others.

There are people in your life that have hurt you. There are instances that probably live in your mind. At times the hurt can overtake you. That's usually when something else happens that reminds you of the pain that person caused you. I know it is difficult to let our feelings go. We want justice; we want vindication; we would give anything for an apology. There's a big problem with that type of living though. It assumes that we have never done anything wrong ourselves, and that's just not the way it is. On numerous occasions, we were in the wrong and had to apologize. We've had lots of moments when we did not get things right. How can we, who have committed the same act, stand in judgment of another? This is an opportunity to free yourself of this cyclic struggle. You may never get an apology and that is okay. I understand that in this instance, harm has been inflicted on you. The pain you carry is great, and what they did to you was significant, but carrying that pain and nursing that grudge every day is injuring no one but you. If you were looking for a sign to let the hurt go, this is that sign. This is that moment. This is the time to let it go. This is the time to forgive those who have hurt you.

Conceivably, they could have spoken the negative words over your life that we referenced earlier. Maybe they are a parent or grandparent that abandoned you. Possibly they are a spouse that divorced you, or a friend that betrayed you. No matter what has been done, now is the time. Imagine the liberty that could be yours if you finally decided to let it go! You have carried this long enough. Think about the freedom you could bring to someone else simply by telling them you forgive them. You have repented for the hurts you have caused and now you are coming to them in humility, not superiority. The effect of that posture can be tremendous.

Think of those in your life that you need to forgive. Write their names below.

I understand that some of you may not be ready for this. This would be a great time to mention that to God too. He understands. Maybe you need to include the people you want to forgive but are not ready to forgive on your list as well, and then ask God for help with that. It's okay. Again, I will be here when you get back.

The Forgiveness List

_____

_____

_____

_____

_____

What we believe about others also affects how we help others. You were created to connect and bring purpose to others. This is counter to the world's message. The world tries to condition you that it is all about you, and all about what you want. That's not true. That is not the way we are intended to live life. Once we settle the purpose question, everything changes. The greatest pleasure and fulfillment you will ever get out of life is through helping others. You were created that way. We spend so much time focusing on our own inner joy that we miss this fundamental truth about our existence. True joy comes from others by helping others. We will talk about that a little later in this book.

So, there you have it. Three areas of life that we must wrestle with in relation to our belief system: What we believe about purpose; what we believe about ourselves; and what we believe about others.

If we are going to find freedom from the struggles of life, what we truly believe in these key areas is the beginning step in our journey, but we are far from done. We have dealt with some foundational issues in this chapter. To be honest, I cried as I typed those words about my own father and had a realization in that moment that I am going to carry with me for the rest of my life. I came to grips with something in this chapter myself, and I hope you did too. Whew! That was deep stuff, and I hate to say it, but I told you I might meddle in your life a bit. If you aren't too frightened, turn the page with me, and let's keep going! I'll be waiting on the other side.

CHAPTER 3

THIS IS WHO I AM

*H*ello, my name is Wendell Brown. What is your name? Nice to meet you. Where did you grow up? I grew up in Alabama. Did you play sports or play in band? I played basketball. Tell me about your family. They sound very nice. I have four children and a wonderful wife. What do you like to do for fun? That sounds like a lot of fun. I love to go on the lake. It is my favorite pastime on earth. Tell me about your job. Is it everything you hoped it would be? I love what I do. I get to help people and I love it. I have one more question for you. Who are you? I know it is hard to answer that question. Wait, before you answer that question, you want to ask me a question? That's not how this works, but okay, go ahead. "Who am I?" Wait, I am the one asking questions here.

The dreaded "Who are you?" question. Why is it so difficult to answer? Perhaps it is because we allow the opinions of others to shape our understanding of our self, instead of defining who we are on our own. Think about your life for a moment. How concerned are you with what people think about you? Do you cut your grass so that your neighbors are happy with your yard? Did you buy that designer purse so everyone will think well of you?

Are you kind to others so they think you are a wonderful person? Are you focused on opinion over reality? Did you try that drug with your friends because you gave into peer pressure? Think about your life. What do you do to maintain a particular image? Think about some real-world examples. That will help you as we work through this question.

If we live our lives to appease others, we are in real danger. This is the natural place to warn teenagers. Teens, absolutely *do not* live your life to please others. Be different and stand out. Yet, do not for one second let adults fool you. We struggle with this just as much as any of you walking the halls of your school, and sadly, we make judgments based on what other adults think of us all the time: decisions about our appearance, language, cars, where we live, our education, and so on.

The "Who are you?" question is also difficult in our society because we have labels for everyone and everything. Think I am making this up? Last I checked, we have over 521 named phobias.[2] We have a label for almost every struggle you can have, but it goes far beyond phobias. Say something the wrong way, and you could be called a bigot, a racist, a homophobe, a feminist, or misogynistic, even if you were simply misunderstood. Want to fit in with society, then wear the right label. Think the wrong societal thought and you can be canceled. The battles we are facing today with social media and thought control are the same battles we have always been fighting. They are just a little

---

2   List of all 521 Phobias, https://thelistacademy.com/en/list/list-of-all-phobias/

louder today. Want to fit in? Then say the right words, look a certain way, drive the right car, and post the right messages in your socials. Fit in, go with the crowd, and you will be accepted. Have your own independent thought, and there will be a price to pay.

In our previous chapter we talked about created purpose. You were created on purpose, with purpose, and for purpose. Since that is the case, then you are your own unique person. You are not defined by society; you are defined by something else. It's okay. You can say it out loud. I know you want to say it: "I am my own person!" Some of you weren't quite sure. Say it again. "I am my own person!" Wasn't that liberating? Try it one more time, and this time say it louder and with more feeling. "I am my own person!" If you were reading this book at five in the morning before everyone else in your house was up, I am sorry, but they needed to wake up anyway.

You Are Your Own Person

Let's take a moment and illustrate this. Did you know that in the history of the world, your fingerprints have never been repeated. In fact, the National Forensic Science Technology Center states that "no two people have ever been found to have the same fingerprints—including identical twins."[3] The fingerprints that grace your hands were formed when you were just three months in the womb. No other person has ever had the hands

---

3   Kristeen Cherney, "Do Identical Twins Have the Same Fingerprints?," Healthline (Healthline Media, January 26, 2023), https://www.health-line.com/health/do-identical-twins-have-the-same-fingerprints.

you have. More specifically, in the history of the world, no other person has had the same physical and mental makeup you have either. In the roughly 117 billion people that have ever lived, no one has had what you have.[4] (Yep, I googled it.) You are your own person, but *who are you?*

Do you like funerals? I know that's an odd question, but what do you think about when you go to a funeral? I don't just think about the family and their loss. I certainly am there to share my condolences with family and friends. I am indeed there to re-member the individuality of that person and to grieve. Yet I have never been to a funeral service where I did not also ponder my own life. Every funeral—without exception—has caused me to contemplate my own life. To evaluate the type of person I am. To wonder, "Who am I and what will others remember about me?" Have you ever thought that way? I am not talking about trying to dictate what will be said about me from those closest to me after I am gone. I am suggesting

> **I AM SUGGESTING THAT WE HAVE THE OPPORTUNITY TO WRITE OUR OWN NARRATIVE BY THE WAY WE LIVE OUR LIVES.**

---

4   Toshiko Kaneda and Carl Haub, "How Many People Have Ever Lived on Earth?" How Many People Have Ever Lived on Earth? | Corrections Environmental Scan, May 18, 2021. https://info.nicic.gov/ces/global/population-demographics/how-many-people-have-ever-lived-earth#:~:text=Discoveries%20now%20suggest%20modern%20Homo,ever%20been%20born%20on%20Earth.

that we have the opportunity to write our own narrative by the way we live our lives.

Perhaps only a handful of you like to write creative stories, but the truth is that each one of us has exactly that opportunity. You were created, you are your own person, and only you can create the story that will be told about you. Does society label you, or do you define who you are? Are you working to please others for validation, or do you know who you are? Are you living so that others feel a particular way about you? Or are you writing the narrative of your life? What values are hallmarks of the way you will live your life? What principles define the decisions you make?

Each day, you have an invisible pen and paper that author the story of your life. What you value and how you live within those values and principles is indelibly written on that paper with that pen. You are the one who defines the way your story is told. Each day another page, each month another paragraph, and each year unfolds another chapter in your story. What does your paper say about your life?

As you look back, there are probably chapters you like and others you wish you could rewrite. Depending on your circumstances, some of your chapters might end in heartache, and others may end in happiness, yet each day is an opportunity to change the ending to your story. Just because one chapter was tragic does not mean that the next chapter of your life cannot be joyous. The definition of who you are determines whether your autobiography has a happy ending or not. Make no mistake about it, each day will offer challenges, but the manner in which your story is expressed depends on no one else but you.

So, back to the Big Question: Who are you? The best way to answer this question is to finish this phrase: I am _____. We will call this your value statement. You may be tempted to answer the question this way: "I am a mother." "I am a father." Or possibly, "I am a husband." "I am a wife." "I am a young adult." "I am a teenager." They may be true, but your answer must be specific to you, and it must include your values. Remember, you are the only you that has ever been. Who you are must include more than simply your gender or role or stage in life. Who you are is much more than what you do. The person you are deep within can only be defined by what you value. Your answer to this question must be distinct and descriptive of your belief system. Your answer must be specific to you, and it must be principle-driven. I have supplied a list of values to get you thinking, but there are many more that can be added. Take a moment and reflect on these values and any others that come to mind. Which values define your life? Which would you like to define your life? Make a list of your top three values.

Trustworthy	Devoted	Responsible
Sensitive	Ethical	Optimistic
Generous	Affectionate	Dedicated
Honest	Assertive	Courteous
Joyous	Brave	Playful
Kind	Calm	Content
Authentic	Committed	Determined

This Is Who I Am

Compassionate   Consistent   Dignified

Grateful   Understanding   Confident

Honorable   Fearless   Ambitious

Independent   Logical   Productive

My Top Three Values Are:

1. _____

2. _____

3. _____

Why did you select these three in particular? Why are they important to you? Answer these questions with definitive answers. It is your life, and this is important work; however, we are not close to being done yet. Now we need to take your top three values and formulate a statement that defines your life. Here are a few examples to assist you as you articulate this statement for yourself.

- "I am a woman who is a loving mother, faithful wife, and devoted friend."
- "I am a responsible man who is a dedicated father and affectionate husband."
- "I am a confident woman who is a principled leader at work and an authentic leader at home."
- "I am a joyous man who is devoted to my family and generous to others."
- "I am an honest teenager who is striving to live an authentic, determined life."

- "I am a person that is responsible for my own actions, optimistic about my future, and compassionate toward others."

Your answer must be specific to you and what you value. The only way to describe yourself completely is to share the proper definitive adjectives. What kind of man are you? What kind of woman? What kind of student? What kind of young adult? What kind of person are you? Think long and hard. Do not focus on what you do. Instead, use definitive descriptions of the kind of character you possess or want to possess. No matter what stage of life you are in, it is never too late to define who you are!

Put this book down for a moment and reflect about who you are. Then come back and write that down. I want to encourage you to pray and ask God to help you define who you are in light of who He is. This is also your opportunity to look ahead to the future, and not your past. It is okay to use this moment to define who you want to be in an effort to move past your mistakes. Remember, we are living our lives with a pen and paper in our hands, so each day provides a new opportunity to write a different ending. This is vital to your ability to live above struggle, because understanding who we are guides our decisions in moments of doubt, temptation, and fear. When you are faced with a compromising situation, your action will be determined by what you have established in this definition. As you daily live your life, this definition will live in your conscience. This definition will provide the connection from your circumstances to your heart. Defining who you are will dictate your behavior. If you commit to living by this statement, it will not only determine what others say about you, it will also determine the happy ending to your story.

What value specific descriptors need to be in your definition? It may take you days to figure this out and get this right. It really is okay. It would be unfortunate to haphazardly write an answer without true personal reflection, so take all the time you need. As always, I will be here waiting until you return.

My Value Statement

I am _____

_____

_____

_____

_____

_____

_____

So, you made it back. I'm glad; I missed you. How did it go? What did you write? Do you know who you are? Do you know who you want to be? Now that you have written the definition of who you are, you need to say it aloud and commit it to memory. How do you feel about it as you read it back to yourself? There is great strength in memorizing and being able to quote it to yourself and others. Doing that will keep it fresh in your mind. Your definition will come to mind when you face critical moments in your life. Take a few more minutes and repeat it a few more times. Memorize your statement as if you are studying for a test in school. The test is your life, and it is pass or fail. Learn it!

Congratulations! You have now done something most people never accomplish. Most live their lives making it up as they go along, but you have decided to live differently. You have decided to live with the end narrative in mind, a narrative you penned for your story. You have defined your values. You are now going to live differently for the rest of your life. For me, this was the moment everything changed. You now have a set of guard rails to guide the decisions you make since you have set the parameters for your existence. Will you commit to live by these for the rest of your life? If you do, no one will ever wonder who you are. You have now specified the answer. You have conveyed the real you! Great job! So, what is next? I am glad you asked.

CHAPTER 4

THIS IS WHAT I DO

To recap, we have learned that to overcome struggle we must determine the cause, we must define our beliefs, and we must understand who we are. Now, let's spend some time defining what we do. Sometimes when we ask people what they do, they tell us how they spend their time: *I am a student. I am a volunteer.* More often though, the answer to that question is related to how one earns a living: *I am a doctor. I am an engineer. I am a mechanic. I am a teacher.* Who we are and what we do are not the same. Our lives are not determined by our vocation. There is much more to us than how we earn a living. Similarly, being a student cannot define your life because we learn in order to go and do. You may have a career (and it may be a great career), but at the end of your life, your career will not be seated around your bedside. Your family and close friends will. You may be a father or mother, and also work outside your home and have associations outside your family too. You may be a student for the moment, but what will you do with your life? So let's look at that question again: *Deep within you*, what do you do?

View this chapter as a continuation of our beliefs about others. Our purpose in making this world a better place is realized in how we connect with others. What do we do? We must make an intentional decision that we need others in our lives if we are to fulfill our purpose and rise above our struggles. That decision supplies help for us and help for others. What do we do? We choose to connect with others, even when it is difficult, and believe me, it can be difficult. People are interesting, but dealing with conflict can be tedious. Choosing to be a friend can be intrinsically time-consuming too, but the fact that it is difficult does not absolve us of our responsibility to maintain relationships. Instead, its difficulty shows how important it is. You were created to have strong relationships with other humans. There is a reason that we feel love. There is a reason we seek affirmation from others. There is a reason we like to laugh with the group. There is purpose in not wanting to be alone. You were created to connect. How are you doing in connecting with others? If you are going to find triumph in your life, you must connect. This is what we do! And for us to get this right, we must be intentional about with whom we connect.

> OUR PURPOSE IN MAKING THIS WORLD A BETTER PLACE IS REALIZED IN HOW WE CONNECT WITH OTHERS.

We can connect with the wrong people. There are probably people in your life that you may wish were not. They are the people that invoke anger, frustration, and disappointment. You have tried to connect with them in a healthy way for years, but they always seem to leave you irritated. Like poison ivy, the more you scratch it, the longer the rash sticks around, and the more open to the possibility of infection and painful it becomes. These people kind of feel like that. You wish the situation were different. You wish you could move past it or have a breakthrough but it never seems to come. It seems to linger on and on and cause you more pain and frustration.

Or perhaps there are people in your life with whom you have a connection that are not helpful to you. When you're with them, you are tempted to do things you shouldn't. You spend money you shouldn't because they are flush with funds, and you want them to think highly of you. You use rude language around them because you know that will resonate with them. You live and speak in ways that you know are not beneficial to you. You seem to have different priorities when you are with them than you have at other times. This is an especially important distinction for those that struggle with addiction. It is okay to recognize that perhaps this friendship is not helping your recovery. There are people that are all too eager to travel down roads we should avoid. In that case, it is better for them to veer off the path while you stay on your own course. (Remember, you set your values and you have a great answer for who you are!)

There could also be someone in your life that influences your thinking in a negative way. Let me explain. If you are happily married, but you have a friend who is not and is constantly speaking negatively about their spouse, that can affect you adversely. It can cause you to question the validity of your own marriage. I am not speaking about helping friends who are struggling and asking for help with their marriage. There is a time and place for being a friend. I am talking about a continuously pessimistic connection. When others are always bereft of positivity, their negativity can hurt you. You may begin to question the attitudes and behaviors of your own spouse because of their suspicions and concerns about theirs. Their negativity can wiggle its way into your relationship too.

Similarly, you could have a friend at work that hates their job. You liked your job until you started connecting with them. In fact, when you look back, you loved your work until the exact moment you began to eat lunch with them in the breakroom. What happened? Their disdain for their job convinced you that maybe the employment you thought you loved was not so great after all. Mark this down: If you spend enough time around negative talk, all of a sudden, you will have a negative walk. Said another way, "Bad company corrupts good character" (1 Cor. 15:33 NLT). If we are going to fulfill our purpose and do the right things, we must recognize the influencers in our lives and be vigilant in connecting with people that share our values.

> IF YOU SPEND ENOUGH TIME AROUND NEGATIVE TALK, ALL OF A SUDDEN, YOU WILL HAVE A NEGATIVE WALK.

There is a difference between being kind and connecting. Often, some of our worst associations are the easiest to create. Have you ever noticed how easy it is to connect with negative people? They are often outgoing and talkative to a new person because they've already run through everyone else around them. All the other positive people are keeping their distance. They already learned to stay away. You will hear others say, "They were so nice at first, until one day I realized that all they did was speak negatively about others." It is important to choose our friends carefully. Think about the connections in your life. Are they positive or negative? If they are positive, foster those relationships; if they are negative, make a change.

One thing to consider is that we should make it our mission to love others. Every person has value and worth, even Negative Nancy or Frustrating Frank. (*If your name is Nancy or Frank, I mean no harm. It's just great alliteration. I am sure you are a wonderful person, and this was for comedic purposes only, but now, I guess it's not funny at all. Go ahead and feel free to place an adjective in front of my first name (Wendell) as a way to get back at me. Whiny Wendell! There, doesn't that feel better? You're welcome!*)

We have already established that every person can have purpose in their lives. To make a change in relation to who we connect with does not mean we write a person off; it simply means that we change how we interact with them. We should approach these relationships based on the change we want to see. Our approach should be to help them recognize their own value and significance. We may notice their significance before they do. That's okay. As a human with a created purpose, we should make a decision to love everyone. However, we love some at arm's length and some in a close embrace. What do I mean? I am glad you asked!

We love some at an arm's length because we aren't sure we can trust them. Picture it like this: We don't embrace them because we are not sure what their hands will do behind our back. We still want to help them, and want to be a positive influence in their lives, but we love them at an arm's length, unsure how they will respond. They may be at a place in their life where they have not recognized their own value and worth. They may not fully realize they have a purpose; as a result, their actions may be hurtful instead of kind. We don't look down on them. (We've all had our unkind moments.) Instead, we try to offer them something different than what they have known. We are justifiably somewhat guarded in these relationships. Our connection with them is not built on trust. For our own well-being, this forces us to keep distance between us. We must keep a balance between recognizing their value and worth and not losing our own values in the process. Is there anyone in your life that needs to be kept at an arm's length relationship?

Then, there are others we can hold much more closely. We can fully trust them, and we know they can trust us. These are the individuals that bring positivity to our lives. These are the people we know genuinely care about us and for us. These are the people that we care deeply for as well. We are fully connected with them in every facet of life. They share our heartbeat and passion. They are walking the same journey we are. We trust them to place their arms around us because we know they would never injure us. We know they would never stab us in the back. These are the people that bless us. These are those that are truly present in our lives because we have connected with them on a deep level. They are our friends.

I'd like to make one more point about how we love others before we move on. It is fashionable today to vent our frustrations about others on social media. Whether we're posting about the clerk behind the counter, the guy that cut us off on the interstate, or the person who used to be our best friend, this action cheapens the other person's worth. We must not choose to belittle anyone on social media. If we don't exercise self-control, we are not being trustworthy ourselves and not valuing that person. It devalues them to gossip about them with a friend too. If you think victory depends on making you look better than someone else, you are mistaken. There is no triumph in this. Overcoming struggle in our life depends on our inner beliefs and values, not the opinions of others. If you can't speak positivity to the world through social media, close your account. If you can be positive, then post even more. The world needs more positivity! It's like the old saying: "If you haven't got something good to say, don't say anything at all."

Embracing Our Friends

If you are going to live above the struggles of life, you need friends. How are you at being the friend you want others to be?

There are two types of people in the world: the *look at me* people and the *look at you* people. It is imperative that we understand the distinctions between the two for us to properly connect with others. Let's look at them together:

Look at You People

Like being around others

Have many people that call them friend

Have help when they need it

See value and worth in others

Find ways to help

Maintain a giving spirit

Make lasting friends

Are content with others' success

Say, "I should call them to check on them."

Look at Me People

Like to have others around them

Call themselves friends of many people

Need help but can't find it

Tell others their own value and worth

Find ways to receive help

Maintain a selfish spirit

Their "friendships" never last

Find a way to make their story better than yours

Say, "They never called to check on me."

Which person would you rather be around? More specifically, which person are you? Spend a moment and think about your conversations with others. Does your speech lend itself to "me" or "others"? If you have leaned toward a "look at me" life, be conscious of your conversation and interaction with others and seek to make a change. Start small. Slight changes will go a long way in making lasting friendships: Ask about their family. Their experiences in life. Look them in the eye and be present as they speak to you. Use common courtesies in your language like: *It was great to see you. I am so glad we got to talk. Let's do this again. I am so glad I got to meet you.* Then check on them afterward. Send them a text. Call them. Message them. It is okay to have to work on this and practice this. It is not hypocritical or superficial to practice this if this does not come naturally for you. It does not come naturally to many. Choosing to live another way is a beginning. It says that you recognize the value and worth of others and are choosing to place them ahead of yourself.

So, what does it look like to embrace your friends? It is trusting them with the vulnerable parts of your life, true, but more than that, it is them trusting you with *their* vulnerabilities as well.

> **EVERY PERSON HAS STRUGGLES, BUT NOT EVERY PERSON NEEDS TO KNOW OUR STRUGGLES.**

Let's be clear here: Every person has struggles, but not every person needs to know our struggles. (I heard you say *amen* to that, by the way.) There are some that absolutely need to know our struggles because they are our close friends. If you are going to live above the struggles of your life, you must be honest about yourself and your difficulties with a real friend. Who is the person (or people) with whom you can be completely honest? Who are the people that can be completely honest with you? The relationship needs to be one based in positivity and not negativity. These are the people you would trust with your life and vice versa. Have you established that baseline with another? Many struggle with connecting because they make assumptions about the trustworthiness of others, assumptions that were never discussed. Those closest to us have established that our relationship is one of trust.

It is that trust relationship that is so desperately necessary in our lives. We need accountability and truthfulness. *We need people who will share with us what we need to hear, not what we want to hear.* When we trust someone, we can receive even challenging comments because we have established a baseline of trust. What do I mean by baseline? Well, since you asked, I will tell you.

A baseline describes an open and honest relationship marked by direct conversation that shows you want to take your friendship to another level. It is a deep conversation of trust. It is the reciprocal conversation that says something like: "As long as I am alive, I will always be your friend, and will always be honest with you when asked." Or, "Because I am your friend, I will never lie to you, and I will do whatever is needed to help you and speak truth to you at all times." Or, "No matter what happens in our lives, we will never question each other's heart." It is the personal agreement that the two of you will be responsive to the needs of the other. It is the deepest level of friendship. Who have you had baseline conversations with? Who do you absolutely believe you can count on? Do they know you feel that way about them?

In all my years of coaching, many people have never had this specific conversation with the people they believe they can count on most. If you have not had this type of conversation with those you call your close friends, this is the time to schedule that conversation and make it happen. Make a list of the three people in your life that you can count on and why. If you do not have three, that is okay; fill in as many as you have. Have you had a baseline conversation with them? If not, this exercise will help you do just that. Put this on your to-do list and share with them why you consider them a deep and close friend. Perhaps this is a person you admire or one with whom you would like to form a deeper bond. This is a great opportunity to place the right people around you. Ask them to make a baseline bond with you.

Baseline Conversation

Name_____

Why can you count on them?

_____

_____

Name_____

Why can you count on them?

_____

_____

Name_____

Why can you count on them?

_____

_____

A Word about Speaking

Remember, this is a chapter about *what we do*. It is important that you share with others how you feel about them. There is so much power in actually speaking these words to each other. Do not let what you feel go unspoken. Share why you are having this conversation with them and share why you feel you can trust them. If you are married, your spouse should be one of your baseline bonds, since you took an oath to honor and cherish each other. If you are a parent, this is the kind of bond you should have with your children. One of the reasons people struggle in life is because they are not sure who they can count on and trust. This conversation ensures that there are people in your close circles that you can rely on. If you need help formulating a baseline bond, here is an example.

> *I promise that I am your friend and will always be there in your life when you need me. I will hold you accountable with honesty, integrity, and trust. I value our friendship and would never intentionally do anything to break the bond we have. Therefore, I will hold our conversations in confidence.*

To enjoy victory instead of being a victim in our lives, we must be secure in our relationships. We must be certain of those we can count on. Conversely, our friends need to be certain that they can count on us too. Remember, your interactions and decisions impact others because there is purpose for our existence. This also will prove vital in keeping your friendships at the forefront of your life. If you find yourself pulling back from your baseline connections, stop and recommit yourself. You made the baseline bond with the other person. They are counting on you just as you are counting on them. If we are going to find a way through our mutual trials, we must be there for each other on both sides.

To overcome struggle, we make a commitment to connect with others. We make it our mission to foster relationships and ensure that others can rely on us as we rely on them. The title of this chapter is "This Is What I Do," so, will you follow through? Will you connect? Will you dig deep and establish baseline conversations?

Have you done something like this already? If so, you have a baseline friendship and didn't even know what to call it! This would be a great time to call your friend and check in with them. When you do, make it a point to tell them you appreciate them and ask if you can help them in any way.

Are you ready for what is next? I hope so. We are going to take our purpose to a whole new level with *focused intentionality*. I have some thoughts for us to discuss. When you're ready, we will begin. Are you ready? Here we go!

CHAPTER 5

HELP SOMEONE ELSE

Jerry and Joanne might have the biggest hearts you could ever imagine. I do not think I have ever met anyone with as generous a heart as Jerry has, and it is part of the reason he means so much to me. Joanne is amazing in her own right and happens to be the classiest southern lady I have ever had the privilege of knowing. I am equally sure that my wife, Tammi, would agree on these two points.

Jerry met his wife when they were teenagers. It was the 1950s, so picture poodle skirts and leather jackets. You can almost see the show *Happy Days* when you think about the particulars of that era. There was a little place called the Campus Grill on Main Boulevard in Winchester, TN, at the time. Driving his old Chevy, with his slicked-back hair and pack of cigarettes rolled up in his sleeve, is Jerry. Filled with confidence, the story is told that Jerry took one look at Joanne, in the back seat of a car, and called out, "Who is that good lookin' blonde?" Apparently, Joanne thought Jerry was an arrogant young man when she first met him. (I wonder why, with that opening line?) Jerry's version of the story is that she looked back at him and thought, "Wow, who is that guy?"

Whichever story you believe is immaterial, as it wasn't too long before they were together. Apparently, she knew she loved him rather quickly, and she knew because of one pinnacle moment. It was the moment that showed how much he cared: Jerry carried her in the rain through a creek bed for more than a city block to keep her feet from getting drenched. That sealed the deal. Combine Jerry's confidence with Joanne's beauty and dry feet, and love was born.

Something else brought them together as well. Both of their fathers struggled with alcohol. Really struggled. Life was fairly difficult for both of these teenagers, but they made a decision that their lives were going to be different. So different, in fact, that Jerry came and rescued Joanne from her house when her father was chasing the children with a butcher knife while drunk. The two got married just ninety days after they met when Joanne was still a teenager. It wasn't easy, but they were intent on improving their lives—and doing it together. At first, they lived with Jerry's grandmother, and paid her five dollars a week for room and board. (Jerry made $15 dollars a week back then.) They honored God and tried to make good decisions. Slowly life began to fall into place. God took Jerry's slicked-back hair and combined it with Joanne's laughter and beauty, and gave them a great life and marriage. They celebrated sixty wonderful years together!

Help Someone Else

Tammi and I came into their story in our twenties with young children. We didn't have much money and had three daughters at the time with our son on the way. The only way I know to tell this story is to describe how we felt. From our first interaction with Joanne and Jerry, we connected. We felt so much love from them that it was life-changing. They had achieved so much. They owned several successful businesses, but they still opened their hearts and lives to us in a way that we had never experienced before. So often, it seemed that Jerry and Joanne were looking for ways to bless our lives and bless our family. They hired me to do some work for them on the side, and always paid me more than I deserved. Jerry had equipment in his shop that I could use anytime I needed it. If I needed a trailer, it was mine. If I needed a tool, I could take it. I remember the first time I borrowed a trailer from Jerry: I had the wrong-sized ball on the back of the truck, and the trailer came loose and broke the safety chain. I was so nervous bringing it back to Jerry, but his response has shaped my thinking about the possessions in my own life. When I showed him the damage, Jerry said, "Wendell, if you own equipment, you have to accept that it will get broken and it will need to be repaired at some time. I don't ever get upset about things like this. If you own things, you will have to fix them. It's that simple." (Talk about a great response to reactive struggle!) If Tammi and I needed someone to watch our children, Joanne was there. She and Jerry became a model for our children. They loved them so much. Once after our kids came home from their house, and we didn't have dessert after supper, our oldest said,

"Joanne gave us dessert every night!" I remember Joanne coming over and teaching Tammi how to make her first Thanksgiving turkey. Joanne was a great cook, by the way.

In the last chapter, I shared that I love to go on the water. Jerry and Joanne had a twenty-six-and-a-half-foot boat that they kept on the lake. They called and scheduled a time to take us on the lake. They made it such a special day for this young family. We spent the whole day tubing, skiing, and riding their jet ski. It was wonderful for our girls and at a time when we didn't have the means to do this kind of thing ourselves. A few weeks later Jerry called me and told me he wanted me to go back out on his boat with him. I did. Imagine my shock when he said, "Wendell, I want you take this boat out, and I want to show you everything you need to know so that you and your family can come use it anytime you want. If something breaks, I will fix it. If it needs something I will take care of it. I am going to give you a set of keys. You don't have to call me and let me know when you are going out. Just use it like it was your own."

This was almost twenty years ago, and I am still overcome by that kindness today. Who does that? Who gives someone open access to their private boat? Who shows kindness in this way? Most people don't act like that, do they? We are living proof that some do. We did exactly as Jerry suggested too. We used that boat and enjoyed every minute of it! Because he modeled that kindness to us, we have tried to repeat that to others through the years.

I mentioned earlier that Jerry and Joanne had their struggles too. Business wasn't always perfect. Life handed them some battles, but they persevered. Joanne passed away in 2019 from a battle with cancer that began in 2005. I remember asking Joanne how she was when she was in the hospital, and she answered, "I am good, Wendell. I am fine." The truth was that even though she was battling cancer, there was no battle going on inside of her. She knew who she was and who God is.

I want you to consider this for a moment. The way Jerry and Joanne loved us had a lasting impact on our lives. It was so marked that I am writing about them in a book. They mean so much to me that I want you to know their story. I think hearing about the way they lived can be a blessing to you. Tammi and I have been privileged to know many wonderful people in our lives, and all of them, like Jerry and Joanne, have decided that their lives, their possessions, and all they are were given to them to help others.

Curiously enough, life was not easy for any of those we would place in this "wonderful person" category. Every one of them had struggles; they all had adversity, and they all had moments in which they chose to be kind to others. Interesting, isn't it? There's a connection between our own struggles and helping others. We sometimes feel that we cannot help others while we are having struggles of our own, but possibly, the direct opposite is true. Perhaps we need to help others in order to successfully overcome struggle in our own lives.

There is no end to the impact you can make if you focus your attention on what you have instead of what you're lacking. More importantly, when you recognize that what you have can be used to bless others, it's life-changing.

I have another mentor in my life, who says, "There is nothing that God hates more than a spoiled brat." I don't know if that is true or not, but I do think about that statement when I am tempted to complain. I think that choosing the path of the spoiled brat blocks God on so many levels. Do you complain about what is happening in your life, or do you find ways to be thankful for what you have? When we are thankful for what we have, we find that we always have something to offer others! When we are working through adversity in our lives, deciding to help someone else can change our attitude. When we are in the depths of despair, it is amazing how helping someone else can transform what is happening inside us. Remember this: You may not be able to change what is happening *to you*, but you can change what is happening *inside* you. Any time you are struggling with life, consider how you can help someone else, and watch your problems diminish. Why? That is a great question!

> **REMEMBER THIS: YOU MAY NOT BE ABLE TO CHANGE WHAT IS HAPPENING *TO YOU*, BUT YOU CAN CHANGE WHAT IS HAPPENING *INSIDE* YOU.**

Help Someone Else

First, helping someone else focuses my attention on what I have instead of what I am lacking. When I choose to help someone, I must rely on what I believe about others and myself. Choosing to help others reminds me that I have something of value to offer others. Let's illustrate this. Take a moment and think of five blessings in your life. For this exercise, focus more on what you have rather than the people in your life. If you feel like you do not have much, perhaps a blessing in your life is time, or perhaps a blessing is the knowledge of something or a particular skill you have. Perhaps you know how to work on cars or are gifted in working mathematical equations. Maybe you have a car that you never drive, that is in your garage. Or an extra $100 dollars you got that you weren't expecting. Whatever it is, it has the capacity to help someone else. Each one of us will have a different list of blessings. Take some time to really think about this and be specific. You may today be struggling with something that's intense right now, but there are also gifts, talents, and possessions for which you can be thankful.

List five below in the first column only. (Don't worry about the second column just yet.)

Five Blessings   Can Be Used This Way

1 _____   _____

2 _____   _____

3 _____   _____

4 _____   _____

5 _____   _____

Look at your list. Why are they blessings? How can each of the areas you listed be used to help someone else? What would it look like if you took something you mentioned above and used it to help another? Take your list, and now in the second column above add a specific way each blessing could benefit someone else. How can they be used? (I'm not suggesting that you give away everything you have to others and leave yourself with nothing. I just want you to recognize that we all have something we can give or do for others, as we strive to fulfill purpose in our own lives. This is meant to be encouraging.) The point is that your blessings can be used to bless someone else.

As you look at your list, who is the first person that comes into your mind with whom you could share that particular blessing? Write their name down next to that number. (Perhaps no one specific came to mind. That's okay. You can still find a way to use that blessing to help someone.) Keeping this question in your mind will help you: How can your blessings bring joy to others? You will be amazed at what happens inside when you choose to live this way! The realization that you have something to give will be life-changing.

Second, helping someone else reminds us that there is good in the world. When we are hurting and in pain, we feel as if nothing good is happening in the world. We struggle to see any good around us as we ponder our own feelings and circumstances. The incredible by-product of helping someone else is that it reminds us that good exists, and it is real in our world. When you feel that nothing good is happening, remind yourself that you bring goodness with you by choosing to do something kind. You will be amazed at the renewed vigor you gain in your life simply by helping others.

Third, there is an interesting concept in the Bible. This expression speaks to your created purpose. Understanding this belief is vital for any that may still be doubting purpose. Here it is: God has prepared good things for you to do with your life. Ephesians 2:10 says this: "For we are God's handiwork, created in Christ Jesus to do good works, which God prepared in advance for us to do." What if the purpose of your life is to bring good to the world? What if you were exclusively created to make your neighborhood, community, or workplace better? You are alive at this point, and at this time, to help someone else's life in a good way, and it was prepared *in advance*. This is a radical concept. There is good God has prepared for you to do each and every day! Before you lay your head down at night, God is already preparing good for you to do the next day. What if you woke up and the first thing you did every day was ask God to show you the good you are supposed to do that day? How would that change your life? How could that change someone else's life?

I pray a prayer based on that passage every day. Here it is: "God, whatever good you have for me to accomplish today, please don't let me miss it." Believe me when I tell you that this prayer is not for the faint of heart. It's a radical prayer and will bring radical change to your life. Every day it focuses your attention on opportunities for good, instead of looking at what is wrong. You will be amazed how that prayer will center your life on others instead of yourself. Imagine waking up each morning and instead of feeling the doldrums of a monotonous life, you experience the adventure of looking for the good God has prepared for you to do that day!

I prayed that prayer one morning just before I took our luggage out to the car. I had a lot to accomplish that day and to be honest, I was dreading it all. I loaded the luggage in the trunk and noticed a few women outside the hotel in the smoking section. As I came back into the hotel, I recognized one of them as she walked back into the hotel. I had just prayed and asked God to not let me miss the good He had for me to do. I couldn't shake the thought that I needed to speak to this woman. So, I turned and said, "You know, quitting smoking was the hardest thing I ever did." She replied, "Isn't it? Everyone in my family wants me to quit, and I want to quit but I cannot do it. How did you do it?" I answered, "I quit through prayer." "Really? Prayer helped you? I have never prayed a day in my life. I have never really believed in God before. Maybe I should try that." Suddenly, her eyes began to water a bit and I could see the weight of the conversation coming over her face. She really wanted freedom from something she had perpetually struggled with for years. "Can I pray for you?" I asked. "Of course, my name is Tina," she replied. I stopped right there in the lobby and prayed with her. As we finished, she looked at me, her eyes filled with tears, and said something I will never forget: "That was the nicest thing anyone has ever done for me."

Now, that was my only interaction with her. I have never seen or spoken to her again. This began with a brief prayer asking God to show me the good I could do that day. It led to a five-minute interaction that ended with the other person feeling extremely blessed in a way she had never experienced before. I don't know what Tina's life was like. I don't know what positive or negative experiences she had. I do know that God had prepared good for me to do that day, and I believe in my heart that I didn't miss it. The good that He prepared was for Tina in that moment. Tina wanted to quit smoking. Tina wanted a change, and God knew it. Tina, who had never talked to God before in her life, had the opportunity to do that. Think about it. Why did I start that conversation, telling her about my journey with smoking? How did I know that those words would affect her so strongly? I didn't! God brought those words to my mind and I followed through. I am not the story here. I was just walking into something God prepared for me and Tina. Tina is the story. Now, I don't know if you have a relationship with God. (I hope you do. I hope you prayed that prayer in chapter 1.) I only know this: God wants your life to bring good into the lives of others. I do know that you have something to offer, and too often we are so focused on what we lack that we lose sight of what we have to offer. Remember the list of blessings you made! Maybe if we use what we already have to bring good to others, we might find that we aren't actually lacking that much at all! What good has God prepared for your life? Choose to follow it with intentionality.

I envision you reading this book in the morning, sipping your coffee and pondering your day. Or maybe you decided that reading this book is better than watching whatever is in your streaming queue. Great! Or perhaps you are reading in your bed right now so you can sleep soundly at the end of the day. (You're welcome for putting you to sleep!) In any case, this would be a good time to ask God to show the good you are supposed to do. This would be a great time to put that prayer into practice. Give it a shot.

> *"God, whatever good you have for me to accomplish today (or when I wake), please don't let me miss it."*

Take a moment and think of your daily routine. Think about the places you visit and the people you casually encounter every day. Where do you go and who do you know? That list might include the guy at the gas station, the barista at the coffee shop you frequent most mornings, another parent at the ballfield, or the person you pass on your way to fourth period in school. The people you encounter on a daily basis can benefit from your kindness, your thoughtfulness, and your compassion.

THE PEOPLE YOU ENCOUNTER ON A DAILY BASIS CAN BENEFIT FROM YOUR KINDNESS, YOUR THOUGHTFULNESS, AND YOUR COMPASSION.

You are probably going to meet them today, tomorrow, or this week. Is there good that God has prepared in advance for you to do? Can you make their life better? Probably, but you won't know until you ask Him.

Here's one more thing to think about in relation to this. This idea comes from a word we don't use very much today. It is the word *steward*. As a verb, the word *steward* means to "manage" or "look after another's property."[5] If what we have is a blessing from God, then perhaps we are stewards of what God has given us. I'm not saying you have not earned what you have received. Many of you have worked hard to have the things you have in life. Congratulations for the fruit of your hard work! It is interesting though to consider that maybe what you possess is there because you have been faithful and that God has blessed you for your faithfulness. If we believe there is meaning and purpose to our existence, then maybe what you have isn't just for you. Perhaps what you have is a gift to be used to bless others too. Think about it. You are stewarding the gifts God has given you.

Yet stewardship extends beyond our material possessions. Stewardship extends to our time, our decisions, even our skills. Is your time solely to benefit you or can you give some of it to help others? Are your decisions only to benefit you, or can your decisions benefit and impact someone else as well? Here's a quick illustration. Do you leave a twenty-percent tip with the waiter because it benefits you or them? Have you considered blessing them more, and leaving thirty percent, even if the service wasn't very good? If we think about our lives with greater purpose, we

---

5   "Steward," The Free Dictionary (Farlex), accessed February 10, 2023, https://www.thefreedictionary.com/steward.

discover that there are ways we can use what we have to bless others in a larger sense. We are always more than just the sum of our lives! If we truly come into this world with nothing and leave with nothing, perhaps what we possess is given to us for the moments we are alive. If that is the case, are we using what we have only to bless ourselves or to bless others?

As we prepare for what is next, I want to take a moment and tell you how proud I am of you. You have made some life-altering decisions, and I hope have gained some life-giving moments too. Now we are going to turn our attention and focus in a completely different direction. I was trying to place myself in your shoes as I wrote this transition to the next chapter, and I wondered what you might be thinking as you read these words. Are you excited or dreading the next chapter? I hope your life is already beginning to flourish. I hope that you are already sensing a change, or that you have found encouragement to continue. There are all sorts of reasons to bail out, to put the book aside and stop reading, but I sure hope you won't. Maybe the next chapter will provide one simple concept that will change the rest of your life. You won't know unless you choose to give it your full attention. Are you ready to move forward?

CHAPTER 6

I CAN WAIT

Is there anything in your life worth waiting for? There used to be this place close to where I lived that had the best apple fritters (and I mean the best) I had ever had. If you are ever going west on I-40 toward Memphis out of Nashville, stop by Dickson Donuts for the best fritters anywhere. You know how everyone claims that the food from their area is the best? Well, the apple fritters in your area do not compare to these! (My apologies to wherever you are from, and no offense to your grandmother's secret recipe, but they wouldn't be as good as the ones I am referencing.) I don't even really like apple fritters all that much, but I loved these. I tried others, and in each instance, I took a bite and threw the rest away. Listen, these fritters are so good that I once drove thirty miles out of the way to buy a few, and it was worth all the extra time. They are definitely worth the wait! There is no substitute for their fried, sweet, warm, and fruity goodness. If you need to stop for a minute and get a snack because you are hungry now, I will understand.

Seriously, what is worth waiting for? Genuinely think about it. When you were a child, you yearned for Christmas morning.

Later, you couldn't wait to get your first driver's license and savored that moment when you drove alone for the first time. Possibly, you waited for your first kiss, and you were excited and nervous, your stomach full of butterflies. You had worked hard to gain his or her attention, and that first kiss was everything you thought it would be.

When you met your soul mate, you had never felt that way before. You had finally met and married the person of your dreams. If ever there was anything worth the wait, this was it! You thought waiting couldn't get any better, and then you had your first child. Oh, my, was that beautiful baby worth waiting for! It is so difficult to put into words how much that child and all your children mean to you today. Then there's that degree you worked years to receive, and now you have a career. That was certainly worth waiting for.

For those of you at retirement age, you saved and made decisions so that you could enjoy these golden years, and you believe it was worth the sacrifices because you are having the time of your life. Your grandchildren are the center of your attention. You wondered if your child would ever figure life out, and now they have a wonderful family and have given you three beautiful grandchildren. It was worth all the sacrifice and the late-night worries to see them flourishing.

What about heaven? Do you think that will be worth the wait?

I know that many reading this wonder if they will ever experience the kind of contentment I just described. If your life hasn't quite ended up with a sense of satisfaction, it's okay. That is why this chapter is here. By the end of this chapter, you will have something to hold on to that will help you wait a little longer and hope a little more, looking at the future with excitement instead of dread.

Why Is Waiting So Hard?

It is incredibly difficult to wait for something we truly desire. Waiting for something you are not interested in or something you dread is not hard at all; but when we have our hearts fixed on something, it is incredibly difficult to wait for it to come to fruition.

Have you ever chosen a different restaurant than the one you really wanted because the line at the one you wanted was too long?

When you were a child, did you ever grab something to snack on before supper, only to have your mom catch you and tell you to quit eating because you would spoil your supper?

Have you ever settled and bought something different than what you truly wanted because you could get this item more easily and quickly?

The desire to be needed is so strong that many will sacrifice what they truly want so they can be happy for an evening. *Have you ever done that?*

How many people have married a person they didn't truly love because they were tired of being alone? Or tired of loving someone who didn't love them back?

Did you take a different career path because you were tired of waiting for the thing you really wanted to do, so you gave up on it?

Giving up on what we want happens all the time. Too often, people settle for less than what they truly want or need because they are tired of waiting. I think we do this all the time in our relationship with God. People settle for less than God's best in a circumstance, and take matters into their own hands because they are tired of waiting on God to move. Have you given up on God because your prayer wasn't answered? You prayed and held out for months, even years, and you never saw a result, so you decided God must not care or wasn't listening? Perhaps even now you wonder if God is real. People settle for less than God's best all the time.

Not wanting to wait also leads us to do things we know we shouldn't do. In these times, we think things like this: *I know God won't be happy with me, but I'll ask for forgiveness later. At least I will be happy right now.* If anyone has ever struggled with addiction, they know how this feels. *I can't wait for my life to be fixed; I just want to forget about the pain right now.* In so many cases, this is how addiction starts. *My life is not going well. I need an escape. I need a fix for what I am going through. I waited before and it didn't help. The thing I was living for didn't quite work out the way I wanted, so I might as well. Who is going to care anyway?*

Let me illustrate. I was a good kid and grew up in a good home. (Thanks, Mom and Dad!) I wanted to play football in high school, but I went to an extremely small school that had no budget for football, so basketball it was. I truly did love playing basketball though and became a decent player. (I have since coached girl's high school basketball to back-to-back state titles as an adult.) I had an opportunity to play in college, but for some reason wanted to prove I could do something more difficult, so I joined the U.S. Army and went to paratrooper school, ultimately landing (pun intended) in the 82nd Airborne Division.

The army was good and bad for me at the same time. I loved the hard work, but there was not a lot of accountability, and I found that out the hard way. I hadn't been concerned about accountability in the beginning because I was doing everything the right way. Remember, I was a fairly good kid. I was waiting for a relationship that I thought was worthwhile, but the other person didn't feel the same way I did. When that relationship ended, I needed accountability but I rejected it. I had placed my future on a relationship instead of placing my future plans in the hands of God. The thing I had been waiting for and hoping in—the thing I thought I wanted most—didn't work out the right way, so I needed a fix. I needed an escape. So, I did things I knew I shouldn't because, in that moment, it helped with the pain I was feeling. I compromised because I was hurting inside. The interesting thing about compromise is that it gets easier each time you do it. I compromised my morals once, and nothing bad happened, so I did it again. One compromise led to another, and in the process, led to a greater need for instant gratification. It snowballed quickly.

Once, as this phase of my life started to unfold, I became extremely drunk and got in trouble in the barracks. The CQ sergeant picked me up from my drunken stupor and made me clean the barracks that I had desecrated. I could barely walk but he didn't care; he stood over me, and made me clean up the mess I had made. Let's not forget that I had joined the army at age eighteen, which meant I was still under the drinking age. I got everything cleaned up, and he let me go back to bed, but ordered me to report to his desk at 8 a.m. The next morning, I reported a minute early, a little clearer headed and with better breath, having just brushed my teeth. As I stood there in parade rest, he told me how he had every right to throw the book at me. According to the rules, he could discipline me under Article 15. He asked me what I thought he should do. I replied, "Do what you have to do, I guess." He answered, "I don't have to do anything. If I let you go, are you going to learn from this lesson? I remember what it was like to be a private at your age. If you learn from this mistake, you can go a long way. Will you learn from it?" Now, who in their right mind, even hungover in that situation, would not have said, "Yes, sergeant, I will learn from this, and I will never do this again"? Anyone would have been tempted to say anything they could to get out of the situation. Given the severity of the infraction, they might even mean it in that moment. I think I meant it in the moment, but the moment soon faded. The CQ sergeant let me off the hook and ordered me back with the unit. I remember all my buddies asking me what had happened. When I told them out on the field outside the barracks, they were ready to give me high fives, but I was frightened that the CQ was watching, so I kept my head down and tried to hide my excitement at how I had just dodged the bullet.

I Can Wait

Looking back, I wish the CQ Sergeant would have thrown the book at me. I think I would have wised up much sooner. Instead, I began to believe that I was invincible. I thought I could get away with anything and that I could beat the system no matter what happened. Letting me escape the punishment for my actions was a kind gesture to be sure, but it didn't teach me a lesson. The pain that was leading to these actions was still alive and well in my life. Compromise started to become even easier when there were no consequences.

Alcohol soon led to marijuana. Marijuana led to acid. Acid led to cocaine and cocaine led sadly to crystal meth for a season. All of this happened because I hurt inside, and wanted relief. I know what it is like to steal. I know what it is like to borrow with no intention of paying back. I know what it's like to cheat to support a habit. I have written bad checks to ensure I could get a fix, all while serving in the army. One of the saddest moments in my life was when I pawned my gold class ring from my high school basketball glory days to get money to party. I remember feeling so empty, like I had fallen so low at the young age of twenty that I was actually letting go of something so precious to me. That fifty dollar transaction helped me for a moment, but it didn't solve the problem. The horrible feeling I had inside me disappeared when I saw the drug dealer that night, but it came back the next morning and felt even worse. This is the problem with instant gratification. Remember the different types of struggles? Well, this was a great example of a responsible struggle. I was choosing to do this of my own free will!

It is difficult to put all of this on paper. I take no pleasure in having you read about those moments in my life. I only hope it might help you move forward with some aspect of your life. I shortchanged the process of hurt and tried to transform it into happiness. I succeeded for a short time relying on chemicals, but not for a lifetime. So, let me ask you the question again. Is there anything worth waiting for?

Instant gratification is the desire to experience pleasure or fulfillment without delay or deferment. Basically, it's receiving what you want when you want it. Instant gratification is the opposite of what God teaches us to practice. He teaches delayed gratification or patience. A thought-provoking command comes to mind: "Be still before the Lord and wait patiently for Him" (Psa. 37:7).

Instant gratification places the responsibility to fix our problem on our shoulders and proclaims that we know best. Delayed gratification places the responsibility on God and proclaims that God knows best. The problem with delayed gratification is that it goes against human desire. We learned early as babies that if we cried long enough, our caregivers would eventually take care of us. As we grew older, we learned that if we threw a fit loud enough, people gave us what we wanted. If we look at the way adults act in our world, including ourselves, we might discover that even though we have grown in size, we still like to throw a fit sometimes to get what we want.

Why is it so hard to wait? Great question! And there are lots of answers.

I Can Wait

We don't like waiting because it is not easy. If the right thing to do was easy, we wouldn't have nearly the problems we have in our world. Doing the right thing in life is rarely easy. It is hard to wait, especially for something we really want.

Age changes things too. It is infinitely more difficult to wait when we are younger. If we think about that a little bit, we can discover why. If you are reading this book and you are twenty-two, the four years it will take you to complete college amounts to eighteen percent of your life. If you are reading this book and you are sixty, the four years it took to complete college amounts to only six percent of your life. Our frame of reference for how long a year takes to complete increases every year we age (you're welcome for that thought by the way). That is why years seem to go by so quickly as we age, and summer seemed to last forever when we were children. It is difficult to wait when we are young. Mark Twain once said, "Life would be infinitely happier if we could only be born at the age of eighty and gradually approach eighteen."[6]

Another huge factor in waiting is uncertainty. We don't know what tomorrow holds, so we think it is better to have it now. Have you ever wondered where some of our old phrases come from? Ones like: "Don't throw the baby out with the bath water" or "Never look a gift horse in the mouth"? You should look up the meaning of some of them. Often, we are repeating phrases

---

6 Mark Twain, "A Quote by Mark Twain," Goodreads (Goodreads), accessed February 10, 2023, https://www.goodreads.com/quotes/349132-life-would-be-infinitely-happier-if-we-could-only-be.

without understanding their meaning. I was doing that exact thing when I came across the phrase, "A bird in the hand is worth two in the bush." That phrase illustrates why it is hard to wait. In other words, it is better to have one thing in your hand of which you can be certain than continue to hope for a greater possibility that might just come to nothing. When we are uncertain, it is very difficult to wait, so we choose what we can get right now to ensure we at least have something.

Additionally, our society makes it difficult to wait. Our culture says we shouldn't wait for anything. Consider how rapidly we can have what we want today: Order it on the app and it's there when you arrive. Connect with a doctor on your phone in seconds—no more waiting rooms. Deliveries can be accessed at pickup locations in sheer minutes. Want a mortgage loan? We can give you a decision faster than a rocket. Anyone remember how revolutionary a video store was? You could hop in the car and go get any movie you wanted to watch. Do you remember getting an un-rewound tape because the person before you hadn't followed the "Be kind, rewind" direction on the sticker and you had to wait to rewind the movie at home before you could watch it? Remember how frustrating that was? Well, now we have on-demand movies and streaming services. No waiting. You can order a car online and have it delivered the same day. We can get information on our cell phones whenever we ask. Want to know what the average income level in your town is? Your phone can tell you. Want to know when it's going to rain? Ask your phone. Want to know what is happening in your community? No need to wait for the news on television, your phone knows.

Information is now. Enjoyment is now. You want it and you can have it *now*! The world says, "Why wait?" God says, "Wait!" The world says, "Experience it now." God says, "Let Me work the experience in you." Can you see how this can affect our lives? When everywhere else in our lives tells us that we don't have to wait for anything, why should we wait for God? This lack of patience leads many to addiction, and much more than that. If I don't like my body image and I buy this product, I will feel better about myself. If I can do this, it may not be what I want but it's better than nothing and it will make me feel better right now! My insecurities, my struggles, my fears, my upbringing, my heartache, will all go away—in an instant.

We all have chosen instant gratification. If you think about it, you have decided to grab a quick fix that ultimately didn't solve the problem at some point in your life. It is difficult to wait, and so much easier to take matters into our own hands. Like the little girl that told her grandmother that she asked God for a doll for her birthday. Her grandma asked her, "I am sure He will get that for you. Why are you telling me?" She replied, "I am telling you now, so I don't have to wait for my birthday. If you get me the doll now, I can ask God for something else."

No one likes to delay the fun they could have now. Why should I wait for God when I can have it now? We often short circuit the great work God wants to do in our lives by seeking answers to our problems in an instant. What if you went on a run one day, and then looked in the mirror and wondered why you hadn't lost weight? How silly it would be to make the decision to quit running after just one run. No one likes to wait for a process to have its result. Having it now is exciting. Waiting is frustrating. *God, I made a good decision today, and I have asked for Your help. Why haven't You answered? I am waiting! God, I am praying, and I have been patient, but God, I am tired of waiting.*

What is the most difficult aspect of waiting in your life?

_____

_____

_____

_____

_____

_____

What are you currently waiting for in your life?

_____

_____

_____

_____

_____

Is there any prayer you have prayed for a long time without an answer? Do you become frustrated when prayers are not answered quickly? Sure you do! Everyone gets tired of waiting.

Everyone. You are in good company. Even so, strength is formed within us as we wait.

> **Do you not know? Have you not heard?**
> **The Everlasting God, the Lord, the Creator of**
> **the ends of the earth does not become weary**
> **or tired. His understanding is unsearchable.**
> **He gives strength to the weary, and to the**
> **one who lacks might He increases power.**
> **Though youths grow weary and tired, and**
> **vigorous young men stumble badly, yet those**
> **who wait for the Lord will gain new strength;**
> **they will mount up with wings like eagles, they**
> **will run and not get tired, they will walk and not**
> **become weary. (Isaiah 40:28-31 NASB)**

If we are going to learn to wait, there are some things we need to understand. God's understanding of your life is inscrutable. What does that mean? *Inscrutable* means that it is "difficult to understand or interpret."[7] God knows you better than you know yourself. His perspective of your life is greater than yours. He sees every angle; He sees every pothole; He sees every circumstance; He sees every moment; He knows what we are thinking; He knows our fears. He knows our doubts, our worries, and struggles, and He offers us His understanding of our lives. God sees the big picture.

---

7 "Inscrutable," The Free Dictionary (Farlex), accessed February 10, 2023, https://www.thefreedictionary.com/Inscrutable.

Think about that for a moment. God offers you an understanding for your life that you don't have. We can't understand God's timetable. We just have to trust in His perfect perspective. God knows exactly what He is doing. It's unfathomable, yet true.

To *wait* means "to postpone, linger, remain, or stay" where one is, delaying action until something happens.[8] You may feel like you can't wait another minute. You may think that there is no value in waiting. You may be at the end of your rope, thinking you will never find the inner strength to continue, yet this fact remains: Those that wait find new strength. The word *new* carries the idea that there is strength for you that you have never experienced before. New strength is literally power you have never known before. Those that wait on God to solve their problems and put their trust in Him will gain a different kind of might and muscle than they had before.

Think about the responsible struggles in your life. Why are they there? Was it because you were tired of waiting? Did you simply want some activity in your life? Were you at the end of your strength? Well, you can gain new strength. When we wait on God, we allow God to make something happen inside of us.

This new strength is strength that doesn't come from us. We could also say it another way: We can't have this *new strength* unless we are waiting on God. You can try it again on your own, but you have tried that before. You can take matters into your own hands or you can wait. The Bible also says this: "The Lord

---

8 "Wait," The Free Dictionary (Farlex), accessed February 10, 2023, https://www.thefreedictionary.com/wait.

is good to those who wait for him, to the soul who seeks him" (Lam. 3:25 ESV).

Consider this illustration of a life cycle that happens in too many people. You can apply this to so many things in relation to our lives. From a new job, a new relationship, a new marriage, a new friend group, a new location, and so on. It all starts with what we will call the Good Season.

The Good Season

In the Good Season of our lives, everything is new and exciting. There is so much potential. We are happy and pleased with the prospects before us. Everything seems to be going well! Good, in fact! We are having fun, and in the beginning, we think this is going to last forever. The new boss you have is way better than the last one. That young man you met—you have never felt like this before. That friendship! Wow! It is so enjoyable to spend time with them. You can hardly believe that your girlfriend actually said yes to marrying you, and now you are married. It is the greatest joy of your life to be married to her. You tell your family that this is everything you ever wanted.

Everyone loves the Good Season of life. Who doesn't love new and exciting? If only it could last forever, but life doesn't work that way. This leads us to the next season of our life, the Bad Season.

The Bad Season

In the Bad Season, what was new has become old. What was exciting has become boring. What was once fun is now monotonous. The new boss you loved won't let you off for the holidays. That young man you met now has bad breath. He didn't do anything wrong, but you're tired now and he needs a breath mint. That friendship hasn't gone well. They hurt your feelings and now you need a new friend. You had so much fun in the beginning, but it's all different now. Your spouse had been the greatest joy of your life, but now you seem to fight a lot, and you are not as intimate as you were in the beginning. Your marriage has become boring, and you start to notice someone attractive at work.

There is the potential for everything in our life that was once good to become bad. Period. What do you do when things become bad? Most people use the bad moments of their life to go back to good, thinking that will ultimately solve their problem. What is good has become bad, so let's get back to the good. It makes sense, doesn't it?

GOOD

BAD

What was new is now old, so I guess I need new again.

What was exciting is now boring, so I guess I need exciting again.

What was fun is now monotonous, so I guess I need fun again.

What was easy now seems problematic, so I think I would like easy again!

Many people live their lives in this cycle. My marriage isn't working, so I need a new spouse. My job became difficult, so I need a new place to work. I am struggling with this friendship, so I need a new friend. I tried what God wanted and even prayed about it, but I am at the end of my rope. I guess I need to take matters into my own hands. I need a quick fix, and now!

What if there were another way to live? What if we worked a problem instead of shortchanging it? We would all agree that we like the Good Season, but have you ever considered that good may not be, well, good enough? What if there were something better?

The Better Season

In the Better Season, we decide to wait. Instead of shortchanging any problem, we wait for new strength from God. We decide to live patiently instead of instantly. We make it our mission to see what God has for us first, instead of taking matters into our own hands. In the Better Season, we will end up thinking things like: *I waited and am astonished at what happened in my life. I thought life couldn't have been any better, but I was sure wrong. I never dreamed it could be this good.*

Life was fairly good for Keith and Rana. They were the all-American couple and high school sweethearts. Keith served in the army, and they married and had two wonderful daughters.

Life seemed to be coming together for them, and they were flourishing. If ever there was a couple in the Good Season, it was Keith and Rana. Yet, like so many things, easy starts to become difficult, and when things get difficult, we have choices to make. It is interesting that most of us do not make poor decisions in our lives when things are going well. Their marriage started to struggle more than they realized and a moment came that changed their lives forever. It came to light that Keith had been unfaithful to Rana. These two had, for most of their lives, only known and loved each other. This one act betrayed all the years of trust they had developed. A Good Season instantly morphed into a very Bad Season and everything changed.

Keith decided that marriage to Rana was more important and asked for a second chance. Rana miraculously decided that she would take him back. Let's note that the decision for both to stay in the marriage did not move their lives back to the Good Season. Far from it. This would be a great place to tell you that the years of trust in each other returned overnight as they decided to truly work on their marriage and let God do a work in them, but that is not how it happened. There were long talks and there were questions. Then, there were more questions. There were harsh words, there was anger, there was frustration, and there were prayers. Lots of them. They

THEY WAITED ON GOD TO DO SOMETHING IN THEIR LIVES THAT THEY COULD NOT DO FOR THEMSELVES.

waited on God to do something in their lives that they could not do for themselves.

Months went by. Years went by. There were moments where they considered quitting, but every day brought a strength to their lives they didn't know. There were moments that brought encouragement to their hearts so they kept at it and did not stop. They continued the conversations, they worked through the hurt, and they waited on God to allow them to forgive. They waited on God to restore trust. They waited on God, and they got new strength. They didn't realize it, but the decision to stay, and the decision to allow God to work in their lives allowed them to move from this Bad Season directly into a Better Season. They discovered that life could be better than anything they could have imagined.

Ten years later, Tammi and I were talking to Rana. I asked, "Rana, how are you doing? How is your marriage?" I will never forget her answer. She said, "My marriage is better than I could have ever dreamed. If you would have told me, when all of this began, that I would have the marriage I have today, *I would relive it all over again in an instant to have what I have today.* You will never know how great things are for us now. I could have never have dreamed life could be this good!"

Good became bad, but Keith and Rana chose to wait on God, and got something better.

GOOD	BAD	BETTER
New	Old	Greater than I Imagined
Exciting	Boring	Breathtaking
Fun	Monotonous	Contentment
Easy	Hard	Natural
Comfortable	Uncomfortable	Effortless
Trust	Distrust	No Doubt

← **Instant Gratification**   **Delayed Gratification** →

We can repeat the same cycles in our lives, or we can choose to work through the problems and allow God to do a work in us. We might find we have something better than we could have ever dreamed. If you are in a bad season, don't hurry back to good; wait for something better!

The Law of the Harvest

There is another way to look at waiting. Let's use an analogy from farming. Have you heard the phrase that we reap what we sow? It means we will receive the crop based on the seeds we plant. The harvest will depend on what is planted. What we miss so often in this analogy is that we always harvest in a *different season* than we plant. The farmers where I live plant in the spring, but harvest doesn't arrive until the fall. It *always* happens that way—*always!* You plant, and then you harvest much later than when you planted the seed. That is the Law of the Harvest.

In our lives, when we make a bad decision we plant a bad seed. Make no mistake about it: There is going to be a harvest for the seeds that we plant. Cheating at work or school is a bad seed, and there will be a harvest for that seed. Having an affair plants a bad seed, and there will be a harvest for that seed. Tell a lie, and a harvest is coming. Continue to compromise your values and a difficult season could be coming in your life. Bad seeds create bad harvests. Our trouble is that we make bad decisions, and somehow think we have gotten away with it. No one noticed, and no one saw, but keep in mind, that harvest hasn't happened yet.

All harvests take time. Many people live their lives thinking that harvest is immediate. They think that if they make a good decision, they should have immediate results. I made a good choice today, yet my life has not changed. I am doing the right things and my world hasn't changed. Why is that? If you find yourself thinking these thoughts, recognize the season you are in. You may be making the best choices today, but *you are planting* a seed that will not have a harvest until later. You can make great decisions now and can plant great seeds today, but you may also be harvesting seeds that were planted a long time ago. Please do not become frustrated, but recognize that as you plant good seeds in your life, a better harvest is coming. You may be in a difficult season of harvest from seed that you sowed or another sowed. Plant good seeds, make good choices, and wait (there is that word again) on God! We must be patient.

I like the way God reminds us of this when He says to us: "Let us not become weary in doing good, for at the proper time we will reap a harvest if we do not give up" (Gal. 6:9).

If you want to live above struggle and find contentment and supernatural strength . . .

If you want to endure hardship and suffering without quitting . . .

If you really want to soar in your walk with God . . . you must wait on God!

There is help for your soul that can only be experienced in waiting on Him. There is peace in praying to Him. I know this season of your life might be bad, but better is coming! What if it were possible to have new strength in your life? What if you could experience a breathtaking life filled with contentment and greater joy than you can imagine? What if it were possible for you to have so much strength that people wondered about you? It is possible! God's strength is made perfect in your weakness.

The Rest of My Story
(Better: The Value of Waiting)

I got out of the army and moved to Florida. While I was there, I wish that I could say that I left all of my addiction behind. I did not. I continued to struggle, but things were gradually different. Many of the concepts for this book were born from the struggles I had and how God worked in my life through them. I remember going to a church next door to where I lived. It seemed like God was talking to me more that night than any other time in my life. I made a decision to put my life in God's hands. It was not an easy choice. It was a decision that required work on my part. It was an acknowledgment that I had failed on my own, and I needed help. I was tired of the loneliness of instant choices and wanted something lasting in my life. I decided that I would wait on Him to work in my life. I remember feeling drastically different inside after that night. I still had struggles, but I was changed. I knew I had a great purpose. I knew there was a plan for my life. All I had to do was trust what God was doing in my life. I have never regretted that decision.

Not too long after that prayer, a woman in that church told me that she had been praying for me and that God wanted her to help pay for my college if I would commit my life to serving God. She was so kind and so giving. She used a blessing she had to bless my life. When I said yes, she gave me a check that paid for my entire first year of college. While I was at college, I met Tammi. I saw this beautiful, curly-headed young lady with a smile that could light up a room, and I was terrified to speak to her. Just so everyone is aware, and, in case you ever meet my wife, she asked me out first—well, kind of. She called me, and said, "Are you ever going to ask me out?" That gave me the strength to finally ask her on a date. God has blessed me through her so much. I read a portion of this book to her last night and she told me she was my biggest fan, and I believe that. I cannot imagine my life without her in it. I am so thankful that God had other plans for my life. God has blessed us with four wonderful children, and more hope than I could have ever known. I could not imagine greater contentment or greater joy. When I think about what my life was and what it is now, I am beyond thankful. I know that I can trust in God. I am filled with contentment that He is in control. Talk about better!

CHAPTER 7

MAKING A DECISION

I f we are going to live above the struggle in our lives, we need to be decisive instead of confused. How can I be intentional when I am not quite sure where I am going? How can I be pragmatic when there are so many points of information? The power of choice is fundamental to our human existence, but how do we make the best choice? There are all sorts of entry points into our thinking today—each with different perspectives on what we do. There are the opinions on television, and sometimes it seems as if we cannot have an original thought about the world without a pundit telling us what to think. There is social media where trending topics can so influence our lives that we find ourselves changing our opinions based on what everyone else thinks. There is all the advertising that seeks to change and shape our thinking in relation to market analytics and messaging. There is our employment where our choices can impact our livelihood. Of course, there are the voices of family and friends, and then there is your own voice and your own thoughts, understanding, and questions. Our own thoughts can keep our life directionally focused, but they can also let us down if they are all we consider. Left to our own, we can find our morals corrupted in ways we would never dream. Then there is the voice of our faith. How do we ask God for help in determining what to do? When do we ask for His help? With all these perspectives and all of these influences, how do we make the right choice?

We are confronted with choices daily. Some seem insignificant and random, and others seem monumental and purposeful. It is important to remember that every choice matters. What do we do? Whom do we listen to? How do we know? There are three voices we should consider when we are faced with a choice. Each one offers a unique perspective, but one voice is truer than any other. The first is your own voice; the second is the voice of others; and the third is the voice of God.

Your Voice

Did you know that when you were created, God gave you an intellect so that you could reason and understand the world around you? That intellect was a gift to help you make decisions. Your intellect has been influenced, as we discussed in an earlier chapter, by the voices that have spoken to you since you were born. However, the choice of what and whom you listen to is yours alone. We are now at a place in this book where you can listen to your voice. You have disregarded the voices in your life that have spoken lies and have listened to the proper voices. You have chosen the right friends and have established a baseline with those closest to you. You have also declared that there is purpose and meaning in your life. You have asked God for help. You can trust your heart. You can trust your perspective.

As you consider a choice, what does your own intellect tell you? Is it right or wrong for you? If you make the choice, what will the outcome(s) be? How will it impact others? What will the result be for you? Note the order when listening to your own voice. The impact for others is ahead of the impact for your life. For us to truly live above struggle in our lives, we have to first consider how our choices impact others. That doesn't mean a person should not do what is best for them, but it is important to consider how our choices impact others before we make them.

As you consider the choice, what does your own experience tell you? Did you make a similar choice in your past? What was the impact? Are you considering the choice based on a want or a need? It is okay to want things in our lives in the proper perspective. The better question is why do you want it?

Take a moment and think of a pivotal choice in your life that you got wrong simply by listening to your voice. Think through the steps that led you to the decision and write the progression below. How did you make the wrong choice?

_____

_____

_____

_____

_____

_____

Most of us can think of a moment where, left to our own devices, we have chosen incorrectly. The great news is that because of our created connection with each other, we do not need to make decisions on our own. Your voice is powerful because it has the ultimate say. Ultimately, you make the decision and will have to live with the results, positive or negative. However, you are not alone. You have others in your life that care about you and can be trusted to help you with your decisions.

The Voice of Others

It should be noted that when we speak of others, we are speaking of those with whom we have a baseline relationship. As we indicated, there is so much in life that is dependent on the voices that we choose to heed. Your baseline friends have established that they are seeking the best for your life. What is their perspective? What do they say about your decision? A great indicator of whether a choice is positive or negative in our lives is whether we want to include those closest to us in our decision. Sometimes, when we are being selfish or are tempted to make a poor decision, we do not want to include the voices closest to us. When you find yourself not wanting to include others, it is a good reminder that you are facing a poor choice. At times, we don't want to include others because we know what they are going to say. We avoid their counsel because we already know that the decision we want to make is not good for us. It is important to recognize our own feelings. If the decision pulls us away from the people we love the most instead of engaging them, we are in danger of making a bad decision. Stop and evaluate why.

When you do include others, it is a definite indicator that the choice you are facing will move your life toward a positive outcome, even if the choice is difficult in the moment. No person has all the answers he or she needs, so the inclusion of others ensures real-life, real-time assistance at our point of need from people that we trust.

A word about those who are baseline friends. When you are consulted and included in the decision-making of others, it is your responsibility to be honest with them. It does them no good if you just provide an answer they want to hear instead of providing an answer they need to hear. If you are in a baseline friendship with others, it is your duty to say what is best for them. This kind of honesty should never be an issue. If it is, then one of you is not living up to the baseline you established in your friendship. I cannot stress how important this is. Here's an example.

Janet had everything going for her. She was smart, beautiful, and a good athlete. She was a leader and people always seemed to be drawn to her personality and charm. One day she met a boy named Greg, who seemed to bring her happiness. However, everything was not as it appeared. She asked her closest friends what they thought of Greg, and they all seemed to voice approval, yet when Janet was not around, they voiced concern over the relationship: "Something just doesn't seem right with Greg," one shared, while another said, "I feel like he flirts with me when he is around me." Janet looked to her family for approval and brought Greg for a family meal. They did their best to like Greg and to treat him kindly, but from the beginning, it appeared that Greg had a different set of values than the family. It was only one meal, so the family didn't seem to be concerned. *Maybe the relationship won't last*, her father thought.

Before too long, things were getting serious. Greg was around all the time, yet there always seemed to be something secretive about him. One of Janet's friends decided not to spend time with Janet anymore because she didn't like the way Greg made her feel. Other friends began to distance themselves from Janet because they weren't sure what to do with a relationship that they knew was not good for her. Janet's outgoing personality began to change. She had been the life of the party, but as the relationship continued, she was becoming more reserved and timid. Her family did their best to like the young man, but noticed the change as well. Her father and mother worked up enough courage to speak to Janet about the relationship on the day she came home and declared they were engaged.

One year of dating passed by with family and friends all feeling as if something was not right, but not one person spoke to Janet about their concerns. Now the couple was engaged. What was everyone to do? Her father and mother finally spoke to Janet, but by this time, it appeared too late. Why had it taken so long? If they were concerned, why hadn't they spoken sooner?

The wedding day approached, and everyone did their best out of love for Janet to share in the day. There were smiles from family and friends for the pictures, but those closest to Janet had no happiness inside. They were sure this was not going to end well. There was no proof, but some thought he was verbally abusive to Janet. Others feared that perhaps it was more. Two years went by, and Janet is at home most of the time. Greg is hardly ever around, and when he does come home, they don't go out. She feels trapped. Her heart is broken as she wonders if she is in a relationship with someone who doesn't love her.

One day, while he is sleeping, she picks up his phone and discovers that he has a dating app. As she looks more intently, she discovers that he has been communicating with multiple women. She confronts him the next morning; he apologizes and says it won't happen again. For the sake of their marriage, she doesn't tell anyone, because at this point, she is quite certain that those closest to her are not pleased with Greg. To tell someone else would further isolate him from her friends, or even worse, isolate her.

Another year goes by, and things don't improve. Greg tells her he will be late coming home from work as he has a career now. She waits for him. Ten o'clock, no sign of him, no phone call. Eleven o'clock and no text message. Midnight and he pulls into the driveway. He walks in and the confrontation begins. "Are you having an affair again?" "Yes, I am, and I'm not ending it," he says defiantly. "I am doing this because I can't stand the sight of you. You are always nagging me, always accusing me. I have had three affairs, and I don't feel guilty. I don't even find you attractive anymore. Look at you. Who would want to stay with you?"

"I am going to leave you," replies Janet. "Where will you go and who will take you?" Greg shouts back as he punches a hole in the wall right next to Janet's face.

A fun, outgoing girl with life at her fingertips is now a shadow of herself as Greg has stolen every bit of joy from her. Why? Because those closest to her were not honest with her. If you are a baseline friend, you have an obligation to share your perspective. If you are a family member, love compels you to speak. It is your obligation to speak truth when you are asked. Of course, all is not lost for Janet. There is always hope, and much that was lost can be restored, but the price she will pay now will be greater than it would have been in the beginning.

I understand how difficult this is. I understand how it is easier to tell people what they want to hear for the sake of peace, but I would contend that this is not love. Love speaks truth even when it is hard. Love shares perspective that the other cannot see. When you have time invested in a long-standing relationship with others, it is your duty to share what you believe from your heart. Your friend or family member can make their own decision, but they need to hear your perspective. Their decision should have no impact on your relationship with them, but it should provide avenues for you to help further down the road should they decide to reject your advice, because they will know when they are ready that you can be trusted to speak the truth to them.

What would have happened to a young lady like Janet, who loved family and valued friendships, if those closest to her had been honest with her? Honest out of their love for her? What heartache could have been avoided? How many wasted years could have been saved? There is no way to know without a proper conversation. We have an obligation to share the truth from our perspective. A faithful friend shares even when it is difficult. They need your voice!

So, how do you speak truth into the lives of those closest to you? Share your thoughts while affirming your love. *It is important that they know you care for them and that the reason you are discussing this with them is because you have known them long enough to see different aspects of their life.*

SHARE YOUR THOUGHTS WHILE AFFIRMING YOUR LOVE.

Be specific about the concern. Why are you concerned? What frame of reference do you have for the concern? Was it something you witnessed? Was it a conversation you had with your friend? To speak truth, you must have a specific concern.

Rehearse what you will say. This will be an important conversation in their life and in yours. Make sure you have thought through what their questions and responses might be. Remember, you know this person and they are close to you, so use that perspective in framing the conversation. If your friend asks for your advice and you are not ready to give it, it is okay to tell them you need some time to think. Reassure them that you need time to think because they are important to you.

Rely on your history for trustworthiness. It is important that you rely on your past together as you frame the conversation. Reminisce with them at key points to remind them why you are a trustworthy friend. Illustrate through your history how much you have loved them and how their friendship means something to you. If you have taken the baseline pledge with them, remind them of the words you exchanged and expressed together.

Continue the relationship. No matter what their response is to your conversation, follow up with them. Call them, text them, meet with them to see how they are doing. Too many friendships are broken because a person thinks, *They know where I stand. They know how I feel. If they want to talk to me, they can call me.* This is not the correct approach. Hopefully you will have prepared enough that a tough conversation went wonderfully well. If that is not the case, it is your duty as a friend to continue the friendship, even if they are angry with you. Remember that sometimes the hardest things to hear are the things we don't want to hear from the people we need to hear them from.

These are two voices we need to heed when making a decision, but there is an even more important one. This voice has promised to give us exactly what we need. All we need to do is ask.

The Voice of God

God still speaks. It may not be in the way we would like, but He does speak. The power of prayer cannot be understated. Further, there is a promise from God to us in James 1:5 that we can hold on to: "If any of you lacks wisdom, you should ask God, who gives generously to all without finding fault, and it will be given to you."

Don't know what to do? Ask God!

Not sure which way to go? Ask God!

Need help? Ask God!

Want to make the most out of a situation? Ask God!

Need a point of view you don't have? Ask God!

Need understanding for your situation? Ask God!

He will help you.

Wisdom is the "ability to discern or judge what is true, right, or lasting; insight."[9]

If we feel like we don't have the ability to make the best decision, God says ask Him, and He will give us good judgment. Ask Him, and He will give you a quality you do not possess. He will not give you just a little either. He will give you a generous helping of wisdom. You will have more than enough good judgment. If that wasn't enough, His promise is that if you ask Him for help, *He will not find fault in you.* He is never going to punish you for asking. Whenever you finally get around to acknowledging your need for God, He is not going to withhold from you because you took so long. He will give you the quality of His good judgment generously because you acknowledged your need for Him.

How do you hear His voice?

---

9 "Wisdom," The Free Dictionary (Farlex), accessed February 10, 2023, https://www.thefreedictionary.com/wisdom.

That is a great question. I am certain that God is free to speak to you and me differently. I have no doubt that He wishes to teach you the same lessons that He wishes to teach me. The way those lessons are learned may be different for each of us. We are different people. We have different backgrounds and different experiences, so the manner that God uses to gain our attention may be different. Yet, I think that there is a simple way to understand how we hear from Him.

Let's review the progression of this promise:

We Lack Wisdom —> Ask God —>

He Finds No Fault in Us —> Wisdom Is Given to Us

God does not want to hold back. There is no stipulation about earning wisdom. There is no indication that God wants us confused. Instead, there is simply a promise that if you ask for wisdom, He will give it. Many of us want a supernatural moment. I am convinced that God does work in supernatural ways, but I am equally convinced that He often speaks to us in quite natural ways. I wonder if we are paying attention.

If we pray and ask God for wisdom, and if God promised to give generously, then we can be sure that after we pray, the ideas that come to our mind are from Him. He made the promise to us. Ask, and the ability to have good judgment will be given to you generously. That is exactly how this works. You ask and He gives generously. That is why this promise is followed with this:

But when you ask, you must believe and not doubt, because the one who doubts is like a wave of the sea, blown and tossed by the

wind. That person should not expect to receive anything from the Lord. (James 1:6-7)

Ask for wisdom and be prepared for God to download some information to you. There may be moments when God wants you to wait. There may be lessons He is teaching you. You may pray for wisdom and God's answer is wait, but that information will be generously given to you and you will be sure of it. God wants you to have what you need. God has no intention for you to walk in obscurity. Until you are solid in your heart and your mind, wait on Him. Be sure that when something comes to you, you should follow through with it. If you are going to ask for wisdom, you must believe

> **IT IS SIMPLY NOT ENOUGH TO ASK; WE MUST ALSO DO!**

and not doubt that God is giving wisdom to you, because if you doubt, you should not expect to receive wisdom from Him. It is almost as if God is saying that if you are daring enough to ask, then be daring enough to follow through on what I bring to your attention! It is simply not enough to ask; we must also do!

What about when you think you have heard from God, but you aren't sure? Or what about when what you think He told you to do seems outlandish or uncertain? Great question. You certainly do not want to doubt what God has told you, but you can also rely on others in your life. Baseline friends, family members, and mentors can and should help us with their own experience and perspective on how God has worked in their lives. There is one other way as well. God can give you help through His Word.

He also says, "Seek and you will find. Knock and the door will be opened for you" (Matt. 7:7). He promised generously, and He will come through. All you need to do is ask! There is a great passage in Hebrews that can also help when you need to make a decision.

> **Without faith it is impossible to please God, because anyone who comes to him must believe that he exists and that he rewards those who earnestly seek him. (Hebrews 11:6)**

If faith is the exact thing that pleases God, then it is our responsibility when facing decisions to evaluate the moment based on faith. Which direction causes us to have more faith in God? Which path forces us to trust in Him more? Since faith is what pleases Him, and since He rewards those who ask for His help, choosing the path that leads to more faith is the correct decision.

Your voice, the voice of others, and the voice of God. Whenever you face a major decision, listen to these voices to ensure you are making the correct choice. The most important voice is the voice of God. Your voice will offer the sound judgment that God gives you, but never listen to your voice if you haven't asked God for His perspective first. It is important that we stop and ask God for His perspective if we find ourselves simply listening to our own thoughts. Asking God ensures that our thinking is in line with His direction for our lives and builds our faith in Him. The voice of others helps provide corroboration from their perspective and can be a confirming voice that we are on the right track.

Making a Decision

When deciding, we should listen to the voices in this order: The voice of God, our own voice, and the voice of others.

If we are going to live above struggle in our lives, these voices will help us live decisive lives in a confused world. When faced with determination, do not let the decision linger for too long. Set a timetable for the decision, listen to these voices of influence, and make the decision. Indecisiveness causes more struggle and inner turmoil. Listen to the voices, evaluate the level of faith, and make a decision. Listen and trust what God has generously given you and move forward in faith. Remember, He rewards faith!

Are you ready to move forward or are you tired? Are you ready to go or ready to quit? We placed some emojis below, so you can respond with how you are feeling at this point. Circle the one that best describes how you are feeling right now. It's okay, I can't see your answer, so you won't offend me.

CHAPTER 8

THE HOPE EFFECT

What is the reality of hope?

What does hope look like?

How can it shape my thinking?

How can it change my direction?

If I hope, will I be let down?

If I have hope, could it change my marriage?

Could hope dictate the kind of parent I am?

If I truly possess hope in my life, could I be more patient?

Would I finally forgive myself for the wrong that I have done?

If I lose hope, can I get it again?

If hope were alive inside of me, could I finally move past the grief I feel in life?

Could I become emboldened to live for today, and not let life pass me by, if I had hope?

What if I had the kind of hope that God promises? Would it change the way I see the future?

The effect of hope on our lives cannot be overstated, but too often hope is the very thing we lose. We search for it and look for signs of its presence. We pray for it, and trust that it will come to us in the nick of time in the middle of our circumstances. Sometimes we wonder if we will ever hope again. Sometimes we feel like hope is only available to others, and we wonder how they have discovered the key to this mysterious force that seems to escape us.

But what if hope never leaves us? What if it is a gift of our relationship with God? If we could truly understand its power, it might change the way we live. The effect of hope is so extremely powerful that it provides comfort in desperate and difficult circumstances. In fact, just uttering the word renews our spirit. Take a moment and just whisper the word *hope* aloud. Say it again. Hope! One more time and mean it. Hope! Just saying the word with intention does something to our spirit.

The importance of hope cannot be overstated, but we must investigate where we place our hope. All around the world people have placed their hope in the wrong direction. They have placed their hope in a marriage, a friendship, an investment, a job, a program, a drug, an education, or a promise. All around the world people have hoped for things, trusted in things, and worked for things that have disappointed them in the end. If we truly want hope for our lives, we need to start at the place where hope will never let us down. Hope placed in any other direction than God is misdirected hope!

Past, Present, Future

Who you are today is not just defined by this present moment. Who you are as a person is also a combination of your past and the expectation of your future. Some even argue that because mankind lives in past, present, and future, it is sure proof of our being made in the image of God, who exists yesterday, today, and forever, as we discussed in chapter 2.

Your life today is the sum total of what is in your past: How you were raised, the circumstances in your life, the actions you have taken in the past. All this combined has made you the person you are today. Yet, you are not just a person who exists in the present and the past. You are also a person who has a future. How you look at your future has an impact on who you are and what you become. If your outlook on life is bleak, then that determines the steps you take, which in turn affects the person you become in the future. If your outlook on life is positive, then that determines the course your life takes and therefore determines who you become.

Think about your past for a moment. List three monumental moments in your past that have made you the person you are today. What are those moments? List the first three that come to mind below:

My Past

1. _____

2. _____

3. _____

Were the moments you mentioned positive or negative? Did you cause them or did someone else? Did they help you or hinder you? Why? Did they create a receptive struggle, a responsible struggle, or a reactive struggle in your life? Take a moment and truly ponder the ramifications of your past and how your past has impacted your present. How often do you think about the events you listed? What affect should they have on your future?

You are now living in the present and reading this book, but even the last paragraph you just read is no longer part of your present now. It is part of the past. When we think about past, present, and future events, the only one of the three that we can truly exert any control over is our expectation of the future. What is in the past is in the past. What is happening in the present, you cannot change through wishful thinking. However, you can exert some energy toward the future!

Sadly, though, many generate all their energy toward living in the past and are unable to work through what happened to them, the mistakes they have made, or the people they have lost. Generating our energy on the past will not change our future. The only way to change your life is to start living for tomorrow, and the next day, and the next month, and the next year, and the next years, and so on. Living your present focused on your past will not change your future. However, living in the present focused on your future *will* change your future. No matter what has happened in your past, every person has a future. Forget what lies behind and focus on what is ahead![10]

10 See Philippians 3:13.

Past　　　　**Present**　　　　**Future**

**Looking back
does not
change your
future**

Past　　　　**Present**　　　　**Future**

**Looking
forward
changes
your future**

As you consider the future, what do you believe your future will be? That is where the gift of hope comes in. At one of my son's first pee-wee football games, his team was losing considerably. The difference in the score was so great that there was no way his team was going to come back. I was on the sidelines helping with the chains, and I asked him how he was doing with losing so badly with three minutes left on the clock in the fourth quarter. He looked back at me and said, "I am great , Dad. The game isn't over. We still have three minutes on the clock, and we can still win!" I have thought about that phrase from a second-grade boy many times because of how it affected his present. In my mind, there was no way they could have won the game, but not in his mind. In my mind, the game was over. But he looked at it differently. There was still time on the clock, so there was still hope, and that hope gave him energy for the present. It affected everything he did. It even helped after the game, as he looked at me and said, "We just ran out of time, but I think we will play them again." Hope! *This great gift enables us to focus our energy on what can be, instead of what is.* Oh, by the way, they did play them a second time and they won!

Hope is a direct result of having a relationship with God. You have a relationship with the God who was at your beginning. A God who will never leave you. A God who will see things through to the end. You have access to His wisdom. You have a front row seat to see His handiwork in your life. You have the ability to ask for His perspective and His power. If that is truly the case, then there is always room for hope.

There is an interesting progression of hope that we should discuss. Here it is:

**We also glory in our sufferings, because
we know that suffering produces**

perseverance; perseverance, character; and character, hope. And hope does not put us to shame, because God's love has been poured out into our hearts through the Holy Spirit, who has been given to us. (Romans 5:3-5)

Suffering produces perseverance. When we suffer, we develop perseverance. When we have difficulty in our lives, something is being produced. Perseverance means not giving up. Not quitting. We could substitute words like determination and resolve for perseverance. When we have difficulties in our lives—when we suffer—we become tenacious and persistent. That is what suffering produces in our lives. I would venture a guess that most of us do not celebrate the gift of perseverance when we are suffering, but maybe we should. When we have difficulty, we develop tough skin. Suffering is developing a resolve in us that will see us through. There is much we can learn from difficulty. Yet it is more than that.

Perseverance produces character. The more our determination and resolve takes root, the more focused we become. That focus directs our lives in ways that impact the kind of person we become. The persistence that develops in our lives because of suffering has now taken root and is developing character deep within us. Our focus helps us decide who and what we are. It is helping define you as a person. It is helping you write the narrative of your life by helping you develop principles and values. Who you are and what you do is forged through persistence and through perseverance.

Character produces hope. The more we understand about ourselves, the more we understand about God, because He is the One who created us. When that happens, we begin to understand how God moves and works in our lives, and hope is the result. We recognize that we do not have to have all the answers. We recognize that there is help at a moment's notice, and because of that, we have hope for our present day. We hope that life can improve. It is not a misplaced hope; it is a hope that is foundational to our existence because we have settled things deep within us. Here's my definition for hope: *A vibrant and alive reality that neither the past nor the present dictates who we are or what happens to us in the future.* How about that for hope? Hope is real; it is not some ethereal and out-of-reach force out there somewhere or in some faraway place. It is there to enable our future to be better than our past or present, and it is within our grasp.

And Hope Will Not Put Us to Shame!

When you place your hope in God, you will never be disappointed. You will never be put to shame. You won't have to hide in embarrassment. When you hope in God, you can hold your head high as you trust for better days. Why? Because God's love is living in your heart. Take a moment and truly think about that. God is there with you every step of the way—every day. You can have hope because He is there, and when you trust in God, your hope is real! I think that is why God gave us so many promises. In fact, there are over 2,000 promises in the Bible. Those promises are there for you to ensure that you never feel let down as you hope in God! Here are just a few:

- I will not forget you. (Isaiah 49:15)
- I will be your God. (Ezekiel 36:28)
- I will forgive you. (Jeremiah 31:34)
- I will bless you. (Genesis 12:2)
- I will heal you. (2 Kings 20:5)
- I will satisfy you. (Psalm 132:15)
- I will teach you. (Psalm 32:8)
- I will deliver you. (Psalm 50:15)
- I will help you. (Isaiah 41:10)
- I will strengthen you. (Isaiah 41:10)
- I will comfort you. (Isaiah 66:13)
- I will restore you. (Jeremiah 30:17)
- I will save you. (Ezekiel 36:27, 29)
- I will not fail you. (Joshua 1:5)
- I will guide you. (Psalm 32:8)
- I am working for your good. (Romans 8:28)
- I will meet your needs. (Philippians 4:19)
- I will guard your heart. (Philippians 4:7)

The future of your life can be different. This process may take some time, but there is always hope for you. Take a moment and reflect on those promises. Ponder the extent of God's love for you and His help that is available in your life. If those promises are for you, why would you ever think your future could not improve? He is there with you, right now as you read this. What would you like to see differently in your future? What are you hoping for those closest to you? Write down three outcomes you are hoping for in your future. Take a moment and pray over them. It might be the fourth quarter, and the score might be so heavily tilted against you that you think you could never see a win, but there might just be three minutes left on the clock, and you just might get another opportunity to play them again.

A Hopeful Future

1. _____

2. _____

3. _____

All right. No emojis this time except this one—because we have *hope*!

There is a bright smile in your future when you trust in God! Please don't ever forget that! We are coming to the end. We are in the home stretch. Now, we are going to tie all the pieces together and give you a checklist for when you face a new struggle. What are the first things we do to ensure that we overcome the moment and find triumph for our lives? We will tie that all together in the next chapter, with a firm trust that every person reading this book can find hope for their life, even when trial finds them! You have come this far, so we might as well bring it to a proper conclusion.

CHAPTER 9

PUTTING IT ALL TOGETHER

The alarm rings at six a.m. Time to face another day. You are feeling confident this morning. It is going to be a good day, you say as you look at yourself in the mirror. You take the dog out, make a cup of coffee, and relax for a moment before the busyness of the day begins. You shower, you look over your agenda for the day, and make sure you are prepared. You give hugs and kisses before you leave. You say goodbye to everyone in the house. You place your bag in the car and off you go, ready to face the day. Traffic isn't too bad this morning. It usually takes you thirty minutes, but you make it in twenty-five, as you sing along to your favorite song. Your morning proceeds as normal. *So far so good*, you think. You stop for a quick lunch and then at 1 p.m., you see a phone number you recognize. You know who is on the other end, and think, *I should probably take this*. To say this is a call you were expecting would be an understatement. You can tell as the person begins to speak that this is not going to be an easy phone call. This is the type of call you must sit down to take. You look for a place to sit as they begin to tell you the news. Their voice is sad and labored. As they speak, your hands begin to shake, your eyes fill with tears, your voice starts to crack: "How did this happen? I had no idea." *Life is never going to be the same*, you think as you hang up. The shock of the moment overwhelms any confidence you felt as you started the day. The news is so heavy that you just sit there. Someone asks if you are okay, but you cannot speak. You walk away and find a quiet place and try to think. This was bad, really bad.

In the minutes that follow, a myriad of emotions flood your mind. You are not sure what to do; you just know life is going to be different. There are questions that need answers, and there are plans

LIFE IS GOING TO BE DIFFERENT.

that will need to be made at some point, but you need a plan of action right now.

Have you ever found yourself in a situation like this? If you haven't, you will. If you have, you know exactly how this feels. What do you do? What is your plan when the struggles of life find you? This is the moment when we put everything together. I have provided a step-by-step guide for you that puts all the concepts we've explored together to allow you to work through any struggle as it is happening. It is my hope that you can use this as a model to help you rise above and find peace and contentment in the midst of adversity.

How to Overcome Life's Struggles

Step 1 - Determine the Type of Struggle

Receptive

Responsible

Reactive

How you respond in the moment depends on the type of struggle. Where is the struggle originating? How should you respond?

_____

_____

_____

_____

_____

Step 2 - Remember the Importance of Purpose

Pray to God and ask Him to help you see the purpose for this moment. Remind yourself that the other people involved in this struggle have purpose as well. What did you hear from Him as you prayed?

_____

_____

_____

_____

_____

Step 3 - Recite Your Value Statement

When faced with a tragedy, you must remember who you are so your decisions fit within your values. Consider your values as you work through your action plan to overcome the struggle. Ensure that your thoughts and your actions moving forward align themselves with your value statement. Observe areas in this situation where you could be tempted to compromise your values.

_____

_____

_____

_____

_____

Step 4 - Connect with Your Baseline Friends

Tell them what has happened. Tell them you are going to need their help. Let them into your life and do not disconnect from them when they seek to help you. Give them specific things to do to help you, or simply allow them to be with you and help as they see fit. If you have specific items for them to help with, write them down below.

_____

_____

_____

_____

Step 5 - Help Someone Else

Remember that even in your own heartache, there are still ways you can bless others. Who do you need to bless? This will remind you that there is still good in the world. What good has God prepared in advance for you to do? A struggle in your life does not absolve you of your responsibility to do good.

_____

_____

_____

_____

_____

Step 6 - Wait

Instant gratification is not the answer. Wait as God works in your life. Remember the seasons of life—Good becomes Bad, but Better is coming. Remember the Law of the Harvest: A different season is coming; the harvest for that season will be dependent on the seeds you are planting now. Keep planting good seeds! What seeds are you planting? Write specifically what you are waiting for.

_____

_____

_____

_____

Step 7 - Make a Decision

Ask for wisdom from God. Listen to these voices in this order: The voice of God, your own voice, and then the voice of others. What decision do you need to make?

_____

_____

_____

_____

_____

_____

Step 8 - There Is Always Hope

What is happening in you *and to you* is building character that produces hope. Because you have a relationship with God, you can rely on His promises. Your future will be different than your present! Thank God that tomorrow is a new day. Record any thoughts you have below.

_____

_____

_____

_____

_____

_____

TURNING TRAGEDY INTO TRIUMPH

I started this book by sharing how much I have always enjoyed stories of triumph. Your life can be a story of triumph too. No matter where you are on life's journey, you have a future that can be different than your present or your past. I do not suppose that the concepts in this book are a quick fix. Turning tragedy into triumph takes time. There are long nights and difficult days; however, there is always hope because God is there for you!

Having directed "Tragedy Into Triumph" since 2009, I know that there are many people who have found their purpose as they look to Jesus. For me, the greatest tragedy would be for you to miss the help available to you. If you have found yourself at the end of your rope, if you have looked for every other conceivable answer to life's problems except to look to Jesus, I hope you will view this as the moment you have been waiting for.

There is real hope available to you, and today is a great day to realize hope in your life. Did you know that the story of Jesus is called the gospel? *Gospel* literally means "good news." There is never a bad time to get good news. The good news is that Jesus loves you and that Jesus died on a cross so that you could have a relationship with Him. He did that so you could receive Him into your life. The Bible says that He is a friend who sticks closer than a brother. Jesus will be there in your darkest moments; all you have to do is ask Him into your life. If you would like to do that and haven't, here is the prayer I offered in Chapter 2:

> *God, would You come into my life and help me discover purpose? I ask forgiveness for anything I have done and want to have a relationship with You. Would You come into my heart and walk the journey of life with me? I would love to have Your Spirit speak to me. Thank You! In Jesus' name, Amen!*

This prayer will change your life and will be the best step you could ever take in overcoming your struggles. Jesus will never leave you, and He will never ignore you. You will never have to search for Him because He will be present at every moment of your life. I have been praying for every person reading this. I pray that God will begin to do a wonderful work in your life as you find hope that is only found in Him. I am so proud of you! If you took this step (or if a concept in this book spoke to you), I would love to hear from you. I can be reached at: tragedyintotriumph.com/books

I want God's best for your life, so if there is any way I can help, I will.

Additionally, if you have an amazing story of how God has brought you freedom from the struggles in your life, we would love it if you shared it with us. You can find all the information you need at tragedyintotriumph.com.

May God bless you as you find freedom in Him!

IF YOU ENJOYED THIS BOOK, WILL YOU SPREAD THE WORD?

There are several ways you can help me get the word out about the message of this book…

- Post a 5-Star review on Amazon.
- Write about the book on your Facebook, Twitter, Instagram, LinkedIn, – any social media you regularly use!
- If you blog, consider referencing the book, or publishing an excerpt from the book with a link back to my website. You have my permission to do this as long as you provide proper credit and backlinks.
- Recommend the book to friends – word-of-mouth is still the most effective form of advertising.
- Purchase additional copies to give away as gifts.

If something great happened to you as you read this book, please send me a message and let me know. I want to celebrate with you. The best way to send me a message is to visit

www.TragedyIntoTriumph.com/books

NEED A DYNAMIC SPEAKER FOR YOUR NEXT EVENT?

Wendell Brown can share his story of encouragement with laughter, passion, and practical steps to help your audience discover ways to overcome life's circumstances and take their next great step in their journey of life.

HOW ABOUT COACHING YOUR GROUP TO WORK AS A TEAM AND OVERCOME ADVERSITY?

For over 20 years, Wendell has been leading boards, employees, and groups by building teams, establishing direction, and helping organizations navigate through difficult circumstances to flourish in their mission.

NEED A PERSONAL DYNAMIC COACH?

Wendell can provide one-on-one coaching to help you determine direction, overcome adversity, and be the best version of yourself.

If you would like to submit a speaking/coaching request, please do so by visiting: TragedyIntoTriumph.com/speaking